ESOL

Practice Grammar

Supplementary Grammar Support for ESOL Students

ENTRY LEVELS 1–2

DAVID KING

Published by
Garnet Publishing Ltd.
8 Southern Court
South Street
Reading RG1 4QS, UK

www.garneteducation.com

ISBN 978 1 85964 472 0

British Library Cataloguing-in-Publication Data
A catalogue record for this book is available from the British Library.

Production

Project manager:	*Simone Davies*
Project consultant:	*Rod Webb*
Editorial team:	*Kate Brown, Simone Davies, Lynn Thomson*
Design:	*Christin Helen Auth, Mike Hinks*
Layout:	*Christin Helen Auth*
Illustration:	*Doug Nash*

Every effort has been made to trace the copyright holders and we apologize in advance for any unintentional omissions. We will be happy to insert the appropriate acknowledgements in any subsequent editions.

Printed and bound
in Lebanon by International Press

Who is it for?

The book is designed primarily, but not exclusively, for adult students studying ESOL at schools and colleges in the United Kingdom.

It can be used to support topic- and function-based class work. Alternatively, students can use it for self-study or for their own reference.

The rationale underlying the book is to make grammar accessible, relevant and memorable. This is done by making use of step-by-step activities and clear contextualized language.

Level

The material takes the Key Grammatical Structures at Entry Levels 1/2 from the Adult ESOL core curriculum as its basis.

We know that the language profile of ESOL students at or around 'pre-intermediate' level is rarely an exact match for the Adult ESOL core curriculum level specifications. The book therefore attempts to take this 'spiky profile' of ESOL classes into account through accessible explanations and graded practice exercises.

Content

The book contains 30 units, followed by grammar notes, a database containing vocabulary notes and other information, an answer key and a pronunciation key.

Approach

The approach used in ESOL Practice Grammar *asks students to infer the pattern or rule from context, rather than making overt statements about the language, to encourage genuine language development.*

The 'Use in Context' section in each unit presents the grammar point through a realistic scenario, usually a naturalistic dialogue involving characters that ESOL students can identify with. Students are asked to focus on key elements of the language to help them understand the pattern or rule. Further clarification is provided by referring the students to appropriate grammar notes at the back of the book.

A set of exercises practising the grammar point follows each 'Use in Context'. These exercises are designed to account for differentiation within a class by offering a progressive degree of challenge. Where appropriate, the final exercise personalizes the grammar point with communicative interaction.

I would like to thank Sue Messenger and the ESOL students and teachers in the Skills for Life Department at Central Sussex College. Also thanks to Lin for her support throughout.

The writing of a book like this necessarily involves reference to the corpus of published ELT grammar books. In this respect, I would like to acknowledge in particular the work of R Murphy (CUP) and D Beaumont (Macmillan/Heinemann).

David King
Author

1 am / is / are

the verb be 1

Database 8, 14, 15

Use in context

Read about Deva.

"Hi, my name's Deva. I'm from Sri Lanka. I'm 32 years old and I'm married. I work at the local supermarket – today I'm on the checkout but I'm not there every day. My husband's name's Rafiq. He's 36 and he's a taxi driver. We are a small family of four people. Our son is eight and our little girl is only five. Our families aren't in England – they're in Sri Lanka. Sometimes life isn't easy but we're happy."

How do we use am / is / are? (page 96)

A Complete this table and then check your answers on page 123.

	Verb be long form	Verb be short form	Negative form
I	I am	______	I'm not
You	You are	You're	______ ______ / You're not
He	______ ______	He's	He isn't
She	She is	______	She isn't
It	______ ______	It's	______ ______
We	We are	______	We aren't / We're not
They	______ ______	They're	______ ______ / ______ ______

B Complete this table with answers to the questions.

Question	Answers
Are you happy?	Yes, I am.
Are you single?	No, I'm not.
Are you a student?	Yes, ______ ______.
Are you English?	No, ______ ______.
How old are you?	I'm ______.
Where are you from?	______ from ______.
Is your friend English?	Yes, she is.
Is your friend single?	No, ______ ______.
Is your car new?	No, it ______.
Is your car very old?	Yes, ______ ______.
Are your children very young?	Yes, they ______.
Are your parents in England?	No, ______ ______.

Practice

1 Circle the correct option.

They isn't / aren't American.

a *I'm not / I amn't married.*
b *Food in England isn't / aren't cheap.*
c *The teacher is / are ill today.*
d *My name am / is Magda.*
e *The weather in England isn't / aren't very hot.*
f *Buses and trains in England isn't / aren't cheap.*
g *I'm / I is sorry I'm / I is late.*
h *My girlfriend has / is 22 years old.*
i *We're / We'm students at the college.*
j *Is / Are your friend English?*
k *What is / are the capital city of your country?*

2 Match the questions on the left with their answers on the right.

a *What's your name?*
b *Are you English?*
c *Where are you from?*
d *How old are you?*
e *Are you single?*
f *What's your job?*
g *Who is this?*
h *What's her nationality?*
i *What's your address?*

1 *I'm a chef.*
2 *This is my wife, Nasra.*
3 *I'm 31.*
4 *No, I'm married.*
5 *It's 34a Park Street.*
6 *I'm from Turkey.*
7 *She's Syrian.*
8 *My name's Ismail.*
9 *No, I'm not.*

3 Write the correct form of *be*.

"Hello, my name's Myra. I **(a)** ______ *a student in an English class at the local college. My English* **(b)** ______ *very good, but I like my class because my teacher* **(c)** ______ *very nice! I* **(d)** ______ *36 years old and I* **(e)** ______ *from Pakistan. I* **(f)** ______ *not single, I* **(g)** ______ *married. My husband's name* **(h)** ______ *Amir. He* **(i)** ______ *40 and he* **(j)** ______ *a driver for a supermarket. Our children's names* **(k)** ______ *Adel and Answa. They* **(l)** ______ *pupils at the local primary school. They* **(m)** ______ *good at English – much better than me! We* **(n)** ______ *very rich but we* **(o)** ______ *happy!"*

4 Work with a classmate. Talk about yourself, your friends and family. For example:

A: *My name's Youssef. I'm 28 and I'm a cook. What's your job?*

B: *I'm a bus driver.*

2 there is / there are / it is / they are the verb *be* 2

Database 12

Use in context

Cheng
There are always lots of cars parked in our street.

Cheng is talking about the street where he lives.

"I live in a busy street near the city centre. There are lots of families with young children in our street. They are all very friendly. At the end of the road there are some shops. There's a supermarket. It's a big shop with everything I need. There's a pub and a café. There's also a post office and a cash point. There isn't a cinema near my house but there's a big one in the city centre, so it isn't far. There are always lots of cars parked in our street. It's a big problem."

When do we use there is / there are / it is / they are? (page 96)

A Complete these sentences.

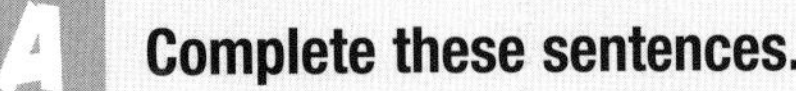

1 ________ lots of families with young children in our street.

2 ________ all very friendly.

3 ________ a supermarket.

4 ________ a big shop with everything I need.

1
CAFÉ

2

B Look at the pictures and answer the questions using there are.

Are there any shops in picture 1?

____

Are there any shops in picture 2?

____

Practice

1 Circle the correct option.

There (is) / are a sandwich in the fridge.

a *There is / are a car outside.*

b *There is / are three eggs in the fridge.*

c *There is / are some / any new students in our class.*

d *There isn't / aren't a phone in my flat.*

e *There isn't / aren't some / any shops near here.*

f *There's / There are some / any people in the office.*

g *Are / Is there some / any good films on at the cinema?*

2 Look at the picture and make sentences with there is / there are.

keys	*television*	*photo*	*book*	*glasses*	*trainers*	*mobile phone*	*DVDs*

There's a television *in the corner.*

a ________________________________ *on the wall.*

b ________________________________ *on the television.*

c ________________________________ *under the chair.*

d ________________________________ *on the table.*

e ________________________________ *under the table.*

f ________________________________ *on the floor.*

g ________________________________ *under the television.*

3 Match the sentences.

a *There's a TV in my bedroom.*
b *There's a bus stop at the end of this road.*
c *There are some people outside.*
d *There are some keys on the floor.*
e *There are only four women in my class.*
f *There's a post office in the town centre.*
g *There's a boy in the photo.*
h *There's a newsagent's on the corner.*

1 *It's about fifteen minutes' walk from here.*
2 *He's my brother.*
3 *They are very good at English.*
4 *It's a little shop. It sells cigarettes.*
5 *It's not far.*
6 *It's old and the picture isn't very good.*
7 *I think they are police officers.*
8 *They're mine.*

4 Work with a classmate. Talk about the place where you live: the town, the street, and the house, flat or room.

For example:

A: *There's a supermarket in my town. There isn't a cinema.*

B: *Are there lots of young people in your street?*

5 Think of your bedroom. Quickly draw the room and the things in it. Show your partner your drawing and ask and answer questions.

For example:

A: *Where is the desk?*

B: *It's under the window, next to the bed.*

3 The present continuous

Database 1

Use in context

It's Tuesday morning. What are they doing? Cheng is talking. Look at the green words.

Today I'm learning English.

Rafiq is working.

Amir isn't working. He's looking for a job.

Jeya and Deva aren't working. They're shopping.

Magda isn't teaching. She's moving house. It's sunny today. It isn't raining.

How do we use the present continuous?

(page 96)

A

Complete the words in this table.

I am (I'm)	I'm not	learning English.
You are (You're)	You aren't	work____.
He ____ (He's)	He ____	look____ for a job.
She ____ (She__)	She ____	mov____ house.
It ____ (It__)	It ____	rain____.
We are (We're)	We aren't	shop____.
They ____ (They__)	They ____	study____.

B

How do we write the ~ing form of these verbs?

1 shop = shop**p**________

2 move = mov________

3 study = study________

C

Complete these questions.

1 What ________ you do______?

2 ________ you study______?

3 ________ he look______ for a job?

4 ________ she mov______ house?

5 When ________ we eat______?

6 Where ________ they shop______?

Practice

1 **Write the ~ing forms of these verbs.**
speak speaking

a *talk* ________ **b** *live* ________ **c** *work* ________ **d** *get* ________
e *take* ________ **f** *walk* ________ **g** *move* ________ **h** *drive* ________
i *come* ________ **j** *use* ________ **k** *study* ________ **l** *shop* ________
m *speak* ________ **n** *have* ________ **o** *do* ________ **p** *phone* ________
q *go* ________ **r** *listen* ________ **s** *eat* ________ **t** *stay* ________

2 **Complete these questions and sentences.**
What are *you* doing*? (do)*

a *She* ____ ________ *television. (watch)*
b *Where* ________ *he* ________*? (go)*
c *I* ____ ________ *my mother. (phone)*
d *It* ____ ________ *to rain. (start)*
e *Amir is in bed. He* ____ ________*. (work)*
f ____ *you* ________ *the computer? (use)*
g *They* ____ ________ *house this week. (move)*
h *We* ____ ________ *a party. (have)*

3 **Look at picture A. What are the people doing?**

Winston is drinking a cup of water.

a *Naomi* ______________________.

b *Jamie* ______________________.

c *Ali and Malik* ______________________.

d *Dee* ______________________.

e *Jan* ______________________.

f *Beatriz* ______________________.

4 Look at picture B. What are the people doing now?

Winston isn't drinking, he's talking on the phone.

a *Naomi* ______________________.

b *Jamie* ______________________.

c *Ali* ______________________.

d *Malik* ______________________.

e *Dee* ______________________.

f *Jan* ______________________.

g *Beatriz* ______________________.

5 Work with a classmate. Talk about what you are doing at the moment, today, this week.

For example:

A: *I'm learning English at the moment.*

B: *So am I. What are you doing this evening?*

4 I / you / we / they

present simple 1

Database 1, 9

Use in context

Hamid: Do you work?
Cheng: No, I don't.
Hamid: What do you do?
Cheng: I study English.
Hamid: Do you know Roman?
Cheng: Yes, I do. We go to the same college. Do you know Jeya and Deva?
Hamid: Yes, I do. Are they here today?
Cheng: No, they go to work on Mondays and Wednesdays. They work part-time.

How do we use the present simple? (page 96)

A

Complete the words in this table.

I study	I do not (don't) study	English.
You work	You _______ _______ (don't) work	part-time.
We go	We _______ _______ (_______) go	to the same college.
They _____	They _______ _______ (_______) go	to work.

B

Complete these questions and answers.

Do you go to college?

a Yes, I _______.

b What _______ you do?

c I _______ to work.

d _______ you work full-time?

e No, I _______. I _______ on Mondays and Wednesdays.

f What do _______ _______? They work at the supermarket.

Practice

1 Circle the correct option.

What do you do / you do?

a *What / Where do you work?*

b *I don't drive / drive not in England.*

c *Do you take / Take you sugar in coffee?*

d *We living / live in Birmingham.*

e *What language you speak / do you speak?*

f *Where they usually go / do they usually go shopping?*

g *They doesn't / don't eat meat.*

h *A: Do you studying / study English?*
B: Yes, I study / do.

i *We don't / doesn't drinks / drink alcohol.*

2 Put one of these words in each space.

work	*do*	*No*	*do*	*look*	*Do*	*work*	*like*
speak	*don't*	*drive*	*don't*	*go*	*They*		

A: Where do you work*?*
B: I work *in a hotel.*

a *We ________ watch television very much.*

b *A: What do you ________?*
B: I ________ to university.

c *A: Do you ________ apples?*
B: Yes, I ________.

d *I ________ a taxi.*

e *Rafiq and Deva ________ go to college. ________ work and ________ after their children.*

f *A: ________ you ________ many languages?*
B: ________, I don't.

3 Write answers to these questions.

Where do you come from?	I come from Thailand.
a *Do you like the weather here?*	______________________
b *How many languages do you speak?*	______________________
c *Do you like English food?*	______________________
d *Where do you work?*	______________________
e *Do you live in a flat or a house?*	______________________
f *Do you drive a car in England?*	______________________

4 Complete the questions to match the answers.

What kind of food do you like*?*	*I like Chinese food.*
a *Where* ______________ *shopping?*	*I go shopping in the city centre.*
b *What* ______________ *at the weekend?*	*I go out with my friends at the weekend.*
c ______________ *any sports?*	*No, I don't.*
d *Who* ______________ *with?*	*I live with my family.*
e *What time* ______________*?*	*I get up at 7.30.*
f ______________ *the cooking at home?*	*Yes, I usually do the cooking at home.*
g *What* ______________ *for lunch?*	*I usually have a sandwich.*

5 Work with a classmate. Ask and answer questions about the things they usually do.

For example:

A: *What do you do at the weekend?*

B: *I usually go shopping and meet my friends.*

he / she / it

present simple 2

Database 14

Rafiq
He drives a taxi.

Does Rafiq work? Yes, he does. He drives a taxi.

What does Amir do? Amir doesn't go to work. He doesn't have a job. Most days, he goes into town.

What does Magda do? She teaches at the university.

Does it rain a lot in England? Yes, it does.

How do we use the present simple with he / she / it? (page 96)

A **Complete the words in this table.**

He drives He has	He does not (doesn't) drive He ______ ______ (doesn't) ______	a taxi. a job.
She ______	She ______ ______ (doesn't) teach	at university.
It ______	It ______ ______ (______) rain	a lot in England.

B **Complete these questions and answers.**

1 ______ Rafiq work? Yes, he ______. He drives a taxi.

2 Does Amir ______ a job? No, he doesn't.

3 Where ______ Magda teach? She ______ at the university.

4 ______ it rain a lot in England? Yes, it ______.

Practice

1 Write the he, she and it forms of these verbs by adding ~s or ~es.

work works

a *like* ______ **b** *teach* ______ **c** *study* ______ **d** *rain* ______

e *drive* ______ **f** *go* ______ **g** *fly* ______ **h** *learn* ______

i *move* ______ **j** *do* ______ **k** *carry* ______ **l** *read* ______

m *live* ______ **n** *finish* ______ **o** *cry* ______ **p** *listen* ______

q *come* ______ **r** *wash* ______ **s** *buy* ______ **t** *take* ______

2 How do we say the verbs ending in ~s or ~es? Complete the verbs from Practice 1 in the correct category.

one sound

likes, rains, d______, g______, f______, l______, m______, d______, r______, l______, c______, c______, b______, t______

two sounds

teaches, st______, c______, l______, w______

three sounds

f______

3 Circle the correct option.

She teach / teaches at the university.

a *He always come / comes late.*

b *Does / Do Hamid like tea?*

c *Jeya don't / doesn't like her job.*

d *Does she has / have breakfast every day?*

e *What time does he usually gets / get up?*

f *Amir doesn't play / plays football.*

g *When do / does the film start / starts?*

h *Takes he / Does he take sugar in his tea?*

i *My son listens not / doesn't listen to me.*

4 **Rafiq is a taxi driver. Read about his typical day.**

"When I take people to the airport I get up at 5 o'clock, but I usually get up at 7 o'clock. I usually work in the city centre. I have a quick breakfast, drive into the city centre and start work at about 8 o'clock. I usually have a coffee break at about 10.30 and I go to a café for lunch at 1.00. I take about 45 minutes for lunch. I finish work at about 6.00, but when it is busy I work late and I get up later the next day. Sometimes I don't get home until 10.00 and I don't have dinner. I like my work. It's very interesting."

Now complete the text about Rafiq's typical day using he ...

When he takes *people to the airport* (a) __________ *at 5 o'clock but* (b) __________ *at 7 o'clock.* (c) __________ *in the city centre.* (d) __________ *a quick breakfast,* (e) __________ *into the city centre and* (f) __________ *work at about 8 o'clock.* (g) __________ *a coffee break at about 10.30 and* (h) __________ *to a café for lunch at 1.00.* (i) __________ *about 45 minutes for lunch.* (j) __________ *work at about 6.00 but when it is busy* (k) __________ *late and* (l) __________ *later the next day. Sometimes* (m) __________ *home until 10.00 and* (n) __________ *dinner.* (o) __________ *his work. It's very interesting.*

Now write a short paragraph about a friend or family member using the third person. Use the paragraph about Rafiq as a guide.

For example:

She usually gets up at 7.30, she has breakfast at 8 o'clock and leaves the house at 8.15.

____

____

____

____

5 **Work with a classmate. Ask and answer questions about a friend or someone in your family.**

For example:

A: *Where does your brother live?* **B:** *He lives at home with my parents.*

A: *What time does he get up?* **B:** *He usually gets up at 8 o'clock.*

6 Imperatives

Database 10, 13

Use in context

Hamid wants to find a post office. He asks someone in the street. Read the conversation and look at the green words.

Hamid: Excuse me. Where's the post office, please?

Man: Go straight down this road. Turn left at the end and walk to the traffic lights. Cross over and take the second road on the right. Don't take the first road. The post office is on the left.

Hamid: I see. Thanks a lot.

How do we use imperatives? (page 97)

A Look at the map. Where is the post office?

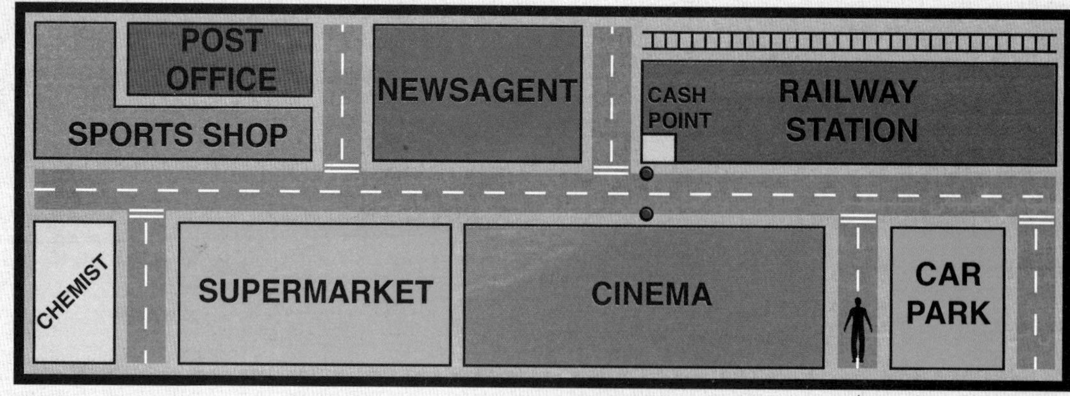

B Complete these sentences with the verbs the man uses in the conversation.

Go straight down this road. ________ left at the end and ________ to the traffic lights. ________ over and ________ the second road on the right. ________________ the first road. The post office is on the left.

Practice

1 Circle the correct verb form.

Go / You going up this street.

a *You do turn / Turn left at the crossroads.*

b *You aren't calling / Don't call me before eight tonight.*

c *Please to answer / answer these questions.*

d *Don't take / You not take more than four tablets in 24 hours.*

e *Finishing / Finish this exercise for homework.*

f *Phone / You phoning me tomorrow.*

g *Please you fill / fill in your personal details.*

2 What are these people saying? Match the pictures with the sentences.

1 *Tick the relevant boxes.*

2 *Don't go near the dog.*

3 *Put the mixture in a bowl.*

4 *Drive carefully.*

5 *Put on your coat.*

6 *Work in pairs.*

7 *Do not exceed the stated dose.*

8 *Get me some eggs, please.*

9 *Turn off your mobile phones.*

3 Put the correct verbs in the doctor's instructions.

Don't go	*Drink*	*Take*	*go*	*Don't get up*	*Stay*	*Call*	*don't eat*	~~*Go*~~

"Go home and (a) ______ *straight to bed.* (b) ______ *in bed for the next 24 hours.* (c) ______________ *if you still have a headache.* (d) ______ *one of these tablets every three hours.* (e) __________ *lots of water but* (f) ____________ *anything solid for 24 hours.* (g) ____________ *to work for a week.* (h) ______ *me if you don't feel better."*

4 Work with a classmate. Ask for and give directions to places on the map. Ask about the post office, supermarket, car park, cinema, cash point, newsagent's, chemist's and railway station.

For example:

A: *Excuse me, where's the post office, please?*

B: *Go straight down this road. Turn left at the end and walk to the traffic lights. Cross over and take the second road on the right. Don't take the first road. The post office is on the left.*

A: *I see. Thanks a lot.*

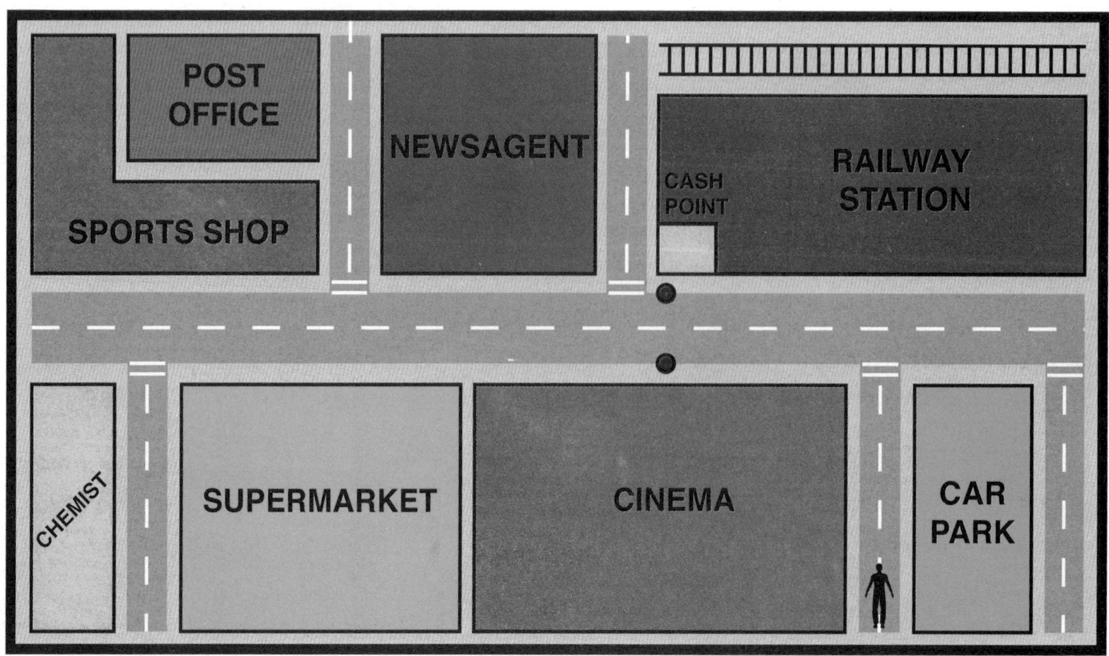

Question words

Jan
What kind of music do you like?

Hamid is in the college library. The librarian is asking him some questions. Look at the green words.

Librarian: What's your name?
Hamid: Hamid Patel.
Librarian: Where do you live?
Hamid: 23 Chapel Road.
Librarian: How old are you?
Hamid: I'm 26.
Librarian: Which class are you in?
Hamid: Class 306.
Librarian: How often do you come to college?
Hamid: Twice a week.
Librarian: Which evenings do you come?
Hamid: Tuesdays and Thursdays.
Librarian: When does your class start?
Hamid: At 6.30.

Jan and Magda are talking. Look at the words in green.

Jan: What kind of music do you like?
Magda: I like most kinds.
Jan: Who's your favourite singer?
Magda: Enrique Iglesias.
Jan: Whose iPod is that?
Magda: It's my boyfriend's. Why do you ask?
Jan: No special reason.

How do we use question words?

(page 97)

A Write the question words.

To ask about things generally: What?

1 To ask about places: ________?

2 To ask about age, numbers or 'in what way': ________?

3 To ask about people or things if there is a small choice: ________?

4 To ask about times: ________? (or What time?)

5 To ask about people: ________?

6 To ask about who things belong to: ________?

7 To ask about reasons: ________?

Practice

1 Circle the correct option.

What / Where do you live?

a *How old are / have you?*

b *Which / What time is it?*

c *How / Who much does it cost?*

d *Why / Which reason are you learning English?*

e *Which time / When does your class start?*

f *Who's / Whose mobile phone is that?*

g *How often / What times do you go to the cinema?*

2 Match the questions on the left with their answers on the right.

a *What's your favourite sport?*

b *Which is your favourite day of the week?*

c *How do you get to work?*

d *When do you start work?*

e *Where's the nearest supermarket?*

f *Who's your best friend?*

g *How tall are you?*

h *Why do you like your class?*

i *Whose car is that?*

1 *My teacher is very good.*

2 *He's called Peter.*

3 *One metre, 62 centimetres.*

4 *Saturday.*

5 *I usually take the bus.*

6 *At 8.30.*

7 *It's at the end of this road.*

8 *It belongs to Rafael.*

9 *Football.*

3 Complete these questions with the correct question word.

Where*'s the nearest post office?* — *In the High Street.*

a ________*'s your favourite kind of food?* — *Chinese food.*

b ________ *big is your house?* — *It's small, only two bedrooms.*

c ________ *mobile phone is this?* — *It's mine.*

d ________ *do you want this job?* — *Because it's very interesting.*

e ________ *do you usually go to bed?* — *At about 11.00.*

f ________ *do you prefer, tea or coffee?* — *Tea, please.*

g ________ *do you do your shopping?* — *In the town centre.*

h ________ *often do you play football?* — *Every Saturday.*

i ________ *is your next of kin?* — *My mother.*

4 Write the questions.

Where do you live? — *I live at 32 Goodman Street.*

a ______________________________? *I'm 27 years old.*

b ______________________________? *I'm a receptionist in a hotel.*

c ______________________________? *I get up at 7.00.*

d ______________________________? *I usually have coffee and toast for breakfast.*

e ______________________________? *I live with my family.*

f ______________________________? *I want to learn English to get a good job.*

g ______________________________? *I prefer the colour blue.*

h ______________________________? *I spell my name H-A-M-I-D, Hamid.*

i ______________________________? *Three days a week, Mondays, Wednesdays and Thursdays.*

j ______________________________? *That's my brother's car.*

5 Some of these questions are right and some are wrong. Tick (✓) questions that are right. Correct any mistakes.

~~Where~~ big is your garden? How big

a *Why do you like tennis?* ______________________________

b *How's car is that?* ______________________________

c *Where does the class start?* ______________________________

d *What's your favourite sport?* ______________________________

e *Who is the nearest chemist?* ______________________________

6 Work with a classmate. Ask and answer questions about your life.

For example:

A: *Where do you live?*

B: *I live in Gossops Green, about 15 minutes from the town centre.*

8 can / can't (cannot) / could / couldn't modal verbs

Use in context

Amir
Can you speak English?

Amir is having an interview for a job. Look at the green words.

Interviewer:	Can you speak English?
Amir:	Yes, I can speak it quite well.
Interviewer:	And can you write in English?
Amir:	A bit, but I can't write very well.

Jeya is phoning the doctor's surgery. Look at the green words.

Jeya:	This is Jeya Perera. Could I make an appointment to see the doctor this afternoon, please?
Receptionist:	Just a moment. How about 3.30?
Jeya:	Sorry, I can't make that. Is there a later time?
Receptionist:	Mm. The doctor could see you at 4.45, or 5.20?
Jeya:	I can't make 4.45 but I could come at 5.20.
Receptionist:	OK, Mrs. Perera, we'll see you then.

When do we use can / can't / could?

(page 97)

A Complete the examples in these sentences.

1 **We use** can **to talk about present ability** – I can speak.
The negative is can't – __________ write.
To ask a question we use can you – __________ speak English?

2 **We use** ________ **or** could **to say something is possible or OK:** __________ make an appointment?
__________ 4.45 but __________ at 5.20.

The form of can / can't (cannot) / could / couldn't **does not change.**

I / You / We / They He / She / It	can / can't (cannot) / could / couldn't	speak English. write very well.
Can / Can't / Could / Couldn't	I / you / he / she / it / we / they	make an appointment? come at 5.20?

Practice

1 Circle the correct option.

I do can / I can swim very well.

a *I don't think she can understand / understands English.*

b *I'm can / I can meet you at 6.00 tomorrow.*

c *Do you can / Can you listen to me, please?*

d *He can to see / see you now.*

e *They can't / don't can come to the party.*

f *Am I could / Could I borrow your pen?*

g *I'm sorry that the dentist doesn't could / couldn't see you yesterday afternoon.*

h *I can / I could use a computer very well now.*

i *Could I ask / to ask you a question?*

2 Complete these sentences with can or can't.

Can *we meet tomorrow?*

a ________ *you phone me later tonight?*

b *There's no more work so you* ________ *leave early tonight.*

c *I'm sorry but I* ________ *help you.*

d *You* ________ *borrow my car if you are careful.*

e *I'm busy right now – I* ________ *talk to you.*

f ________ *you speak up, please? I* ________ *hear you.*

g *I* ________ *get a bus to work but I* ________ *get a train.*

3 Complete these sentences with could or couldn't.

Could *I borrow your car?*

a *It was a shame he* ________ *come to the party.*

b *I* ________ *do it now, if you like.*

c *I* ________ *hear what they were saying, it was so noisy.*

d *A: She* ________ *be late on Monday. B:* ________ *she leave work earlier?*

e *He* ________ *have let me know he was running late!*

f *I'm so tired, I feel like I* ________ *sleep for days.*

4 What are these people saying? Use Could you…? or Could I…?

open / window

Could you open the window, please?

a *post / letter*

b *use / phone*

c *repeat / address*

d *turn down / television*

e *borrow / dictionary*

5 Write questions and answers about these abilities.

play tennis	*cook*	*draw*	*ride a bike*	*play the guitar*
speak a third language	*ride a camel*	*make a cake*		

Can you play tennis? No, I can't.

6 Work with a classmate. Ask and answer questions with can and could.

For example:

A: *Can you play the piano?*

B: *No, I can't.*

A: *Could we meet for a coffee at the weekend?*

B: *Yes, we could.*

9 have got

Database 11, 13

Use in context

Rafiq
We've got a new house.

Read about some people. Look at the green words.

Ismail: I can't go to work today. I've got a bad headache.
Magda: Have you got any children?
Jeya: Yes, I have. I've got a son and a daughter.
Cheng: We haven't got any milk, coffee or eggs.
Rafiq: We've got a new house. It's got three bedrooms and a garden.

When do we use have got? (page 97)

A **Complete these examples.**

We often use have got to talk about:

- ***illness*** – I've got a bad headache.
- ***family*** – ______________ a son and a daughter.
- ***shopping*** – ______________ any milk, coffee or eggs?
- ***things we have*** – ______________ a new house. ______________ three bedrooms and a garden.

I / You / We / They	*have / 've* *have not / haven't*	*got*	*a headache.* *a daughter.* *a house.* *a garden.*
He / She / It	*has / 's* *has not / hasn't*		

B **Complete these questions and answers using have got.**

1 _______ *you* _______ *any children?* *Yes, I* _______.

2 _______ *she* _______ *any children?* *No, she* _______.

Practice

1 Circle the correct form.

I've got / I do have two brothers.

a *They don't have got / haven't got many friends.*

b *He has got / have got a new car.*

c *Do you got / Have you got backache?*

d *Have you got the time, please? Yes, I have got / have.*

e *The house doesn't got / hasn't got a garage.*

f *Has she got a mobile phone? No, she hasn't / hasn't got.*

g *Do you know if they's got / they've got any children?*

h *Has he got / Have he got a cold?*

i *I think he is / has got a dog.*

2 Look at these pictures. What's the matter with these people? (See Database 13, pages 116–117.)

He's got backache.

a ______________________

____

b ______________________

____

c ______________________
____

d ______________________
____

e ______________________
____

f ______________________

3 Complete these questions and answers.

A: Have you got *any sisters?*
B: Yes, I have. I've got *one.*

a *A:* ______________ *any brothers?*
B: Yes, I __________. __________ *three.*

b *A: ________________ any eggs?*
B: Yes, we ___________.

c *A: ________________ a house?*
B: Yes, she ___________. ___________ a nice house.

d *A: ________________ a garden?*
B: No, it ___________ a garden.

e *A: ________________ a girlfriend?*
B: No, I ___________.

f *A: ________________ an iPod?*
B: No, he ___________.

g *A: ________________ flu?*
B: No, they ___________.

4 Complete these sentences with the correct form of *have ('ve)* / *haven't* / *has ('s)* / *hasn't got*.

She's got two cats and a dog.

a *They ______________ a house with four bedrooms.*

b *I can't work at home because I ________________ a computer.*

c *He gets the bus because he ________________ a car.*

d *He's not very well. He ________ a bad cold but I don't think he _______ flu.*

e *We ___________ some milk but we ___________ any bread.*

f *You _________ two phone messages but you __________ any e-mails.*

g *We __________ a new TV but it ______________ a very good picture.*

5 Work with a classmate. Ask and answer questions. Ask about family, things you have, shopping you need or illnesses you have.

For example:

A: *Have you got a big family?*

B: *Yes, I have. I've got three brothers and four sisters.*

B: *Have you got a cold?*

A: *No, I haven't.*

10 some / any

quantity 1

Database 11

Use in context

Ling
Do we need any cornflakes?

Ling and Cheng are going shopping. Look at the green words.

Cheng: We've got some bread, some butter and some tomatoes. We haven't got any milk, coffee or eggs.

Ling: Do we need any cornflakes?

Cheng: No, it's OK, we've got some.

Ling: Have we got any meat?

Cheng: No, we haven't got any.

Ling: Do we need to get some cash?

Cheng: Yes, we do.

When do we use some and any? (page 97)

A **Complete these sentences.**

1 ***In positive sentences, we usually use*** some.

We've got ______ bread, ______ butter and ______ tomatoes.

2 ***In negative sentences, we usually use ______.***

We haven't got ______ milk, coffee or eggs.

3 ***In questions, we often use ______.*** *Do we need ______ cornflakes?*

4 ***We can also use ______ if we expect a Yes answer.***

Ling: Do we need to get ______ cash?

Cheng: ______, we do.

Practice

1 Circle the correct option: some or any.

We've got (some) / any eggs.

a *There are some / any people in the restaurant.*

b *I haven't got some / any money.*

c *There isn't some / any petrol in the car.*

d *A: Have you got some / any change you can give me?*
B: No, I haven't.

e *I've got some / any work I must do.*

f *A: Can I have some / any more potatoes?*
B: Yes, of course.

g *Don't get some / any more apples. We don't need some / any.*

h *There isn't something / anything on the television tonight.*

i *A: Is there some / any post?*
B: No, there isn't some / any today.

2 This is Amir's fridge. Write some or any. (See Database 11, pages 110–112.)

There is some *butter.*

a *There are ________ eggs.*

b *He hasn't got ________ vegetables.*

c *There aren't ________ tomatoes.*

d *He's got ________ milk.*

e *There isn't ________ chicken.*

f *He hasn't got ________ beef.*

g *There's ________ orange juice.*

h *He's got ________ apples.*

i *He hasn't got ________ salad.*

3 Here is Amir's street. Write sentences using some or any and the words given.

shops ~~cars~~ children playing trees houses gardens cats people talking

There are some cars.

a *There are* ______________________________.

b *There are* ______________________________.

c *There are* ______________________________.

d *There aren't* ______________________________.

e *There aren't* ______________________________.

f *There aren't* ______________________________.

g *There aren't* ______________________________.

4 Complete the sentences using some or any.

I'd like some *fresh flowers, please.*

a *I need to get __________ new jeans.*

b *They haven't got __________ children.*

c *There isn't __________ hot water so you can't have a bath.*

d *You must put __________ new batteries in the radio.*

e *I don't think we've got __________ bread.*

f *A: Are there __________ e-mails for me?*
B: No, there aren't __________.

g *A: Can you put __________ more milk in my coffee, please?*
B: Sure, here you are.

h *That boy is getting fat because he never takes __________ exercise.*

i *A: Do you want __________ cash back?*
B: No, thanks. I don't need __________.

5 Work with a classmate. Ask and answer questions with some or any. Talk about things like shopping, where you live, and your family.

For example:

A: *Do you need to get any shopping?*

B: *Yes, I need to get some fruit.*

A: *Are there any shops in your street?*

B: *No, there aren't any.*

11 how much / how many / a lot / a few / a little quantity 2

Database 11

Use in context

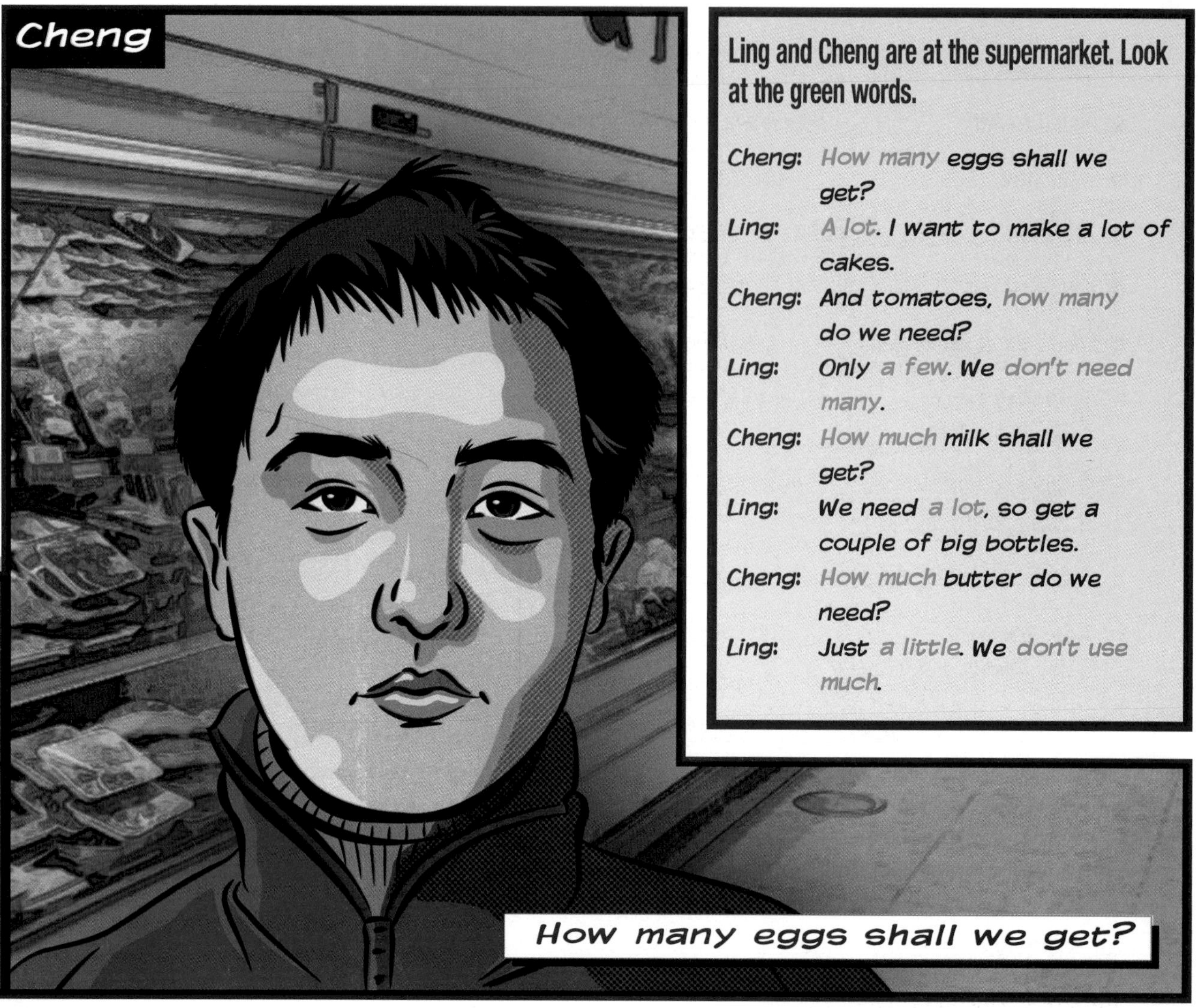

Cheng

Ling and Cheng are at the supermarket. Look at the green words.

Cheng: How many eggs shall we get?
Ling: A lot. I want to make a lot of cakes.
Cheng: And tomatoes, how many do we need?
Ling: Only a few. We don't need many.
Cheng: How much milk shall we get?
Ling: We need a lot, so get a couple of big bottles.
Cheng: How much butter do we need?
Ling: Just a little. We don't use much.

How many eggs shall we get?

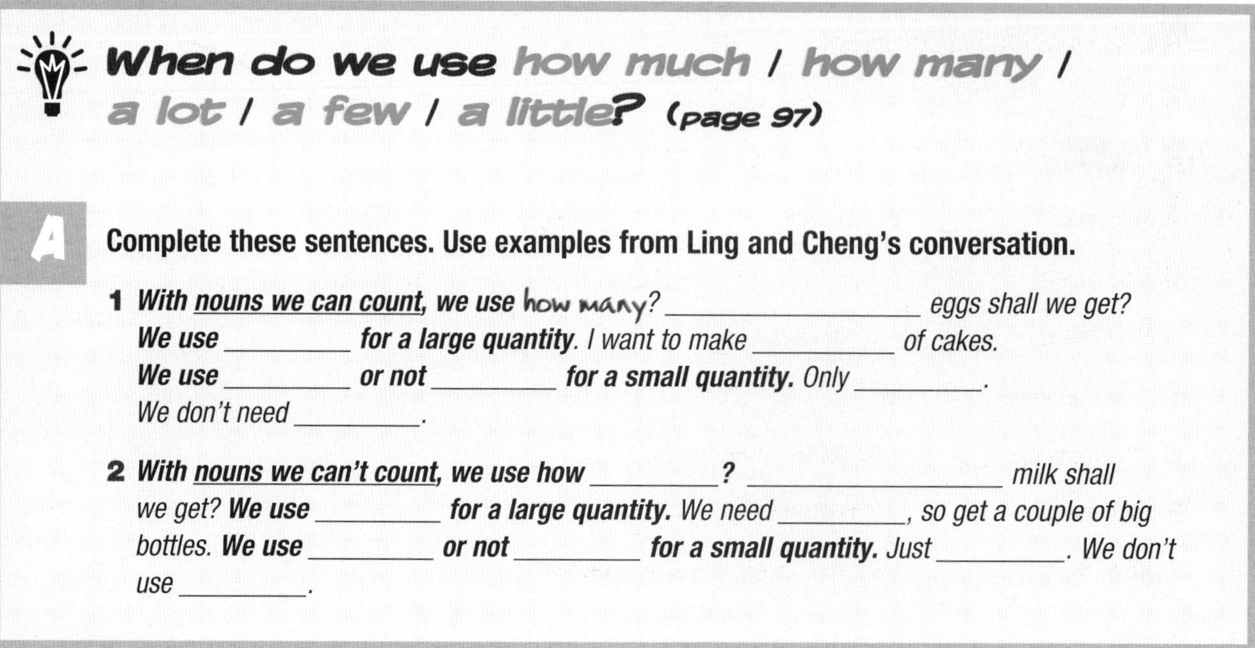

When do we use how much / how many / a lot / a few / a little? (page 97)

A Complete these sentences. Use examples from Ling and Cheng's conversation.

1 **With <u>nouns we can count</u>, we use** how many? __________ *eggs shall we get?*
We use ________ **for a large quantity**. *I want to make* ________ *of cakes.*
We use ________ **or not** ________ **for a small quantity.** *Only* ________.
We don't need ________.

2 **With <u>nouns we can't count</u>, we use how** ________? __________ *milk shall we get?* **We use** ________ **for a large quantity.** *We need* ________, *so get a couple of big bottles.* **We use** ________ **or not** ________ **for a small quantity.** *Just* ________. *We don't use* ________.

Practice

1 Write these words in the correct column of the table.

~~money~~ lessons times time coffee students children petrol tables oranges orange juice cash pounds sugar information English sports sport cola meat exercise onions salad flowers

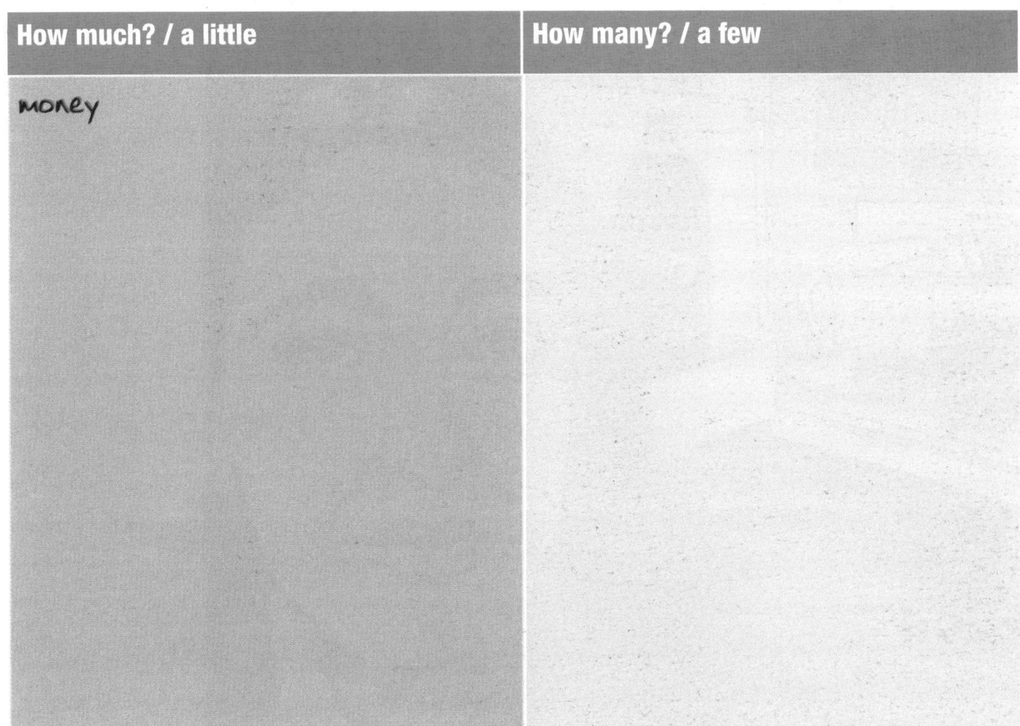

How much? / a little	How many? / a few
money	

2 Complete the questions using the words from Exercise 1. In some cases, more than one word is possible.

How much coffee *do you drink?*

a *How many* __________ *are in your class?*

b *How much* __________ *do you spend a week?*

c *How many* __________ *are there in this room?*

d *How much* __________ *do you know?*

e *How much* __________ *do you eat?*

f *How many* __________ *do you eat?*

g *How much* __________ *do you do every week?*

h *How many* __________ *a week do you go to college?*

i *How much* __________ *do you spend watching television?*

3 Look at Jeya's fridge. What has she got?

She's got a lot of potatoes.

a *She's got a few* ______________.

b *There's a little* ______________.

c *She hasn't got much* ______________.

d *There aren't many* ______________.

e *There is a lot of* ______________.

f *She's got a little* ______________.

g *There are a few* ______________.

4 Write one word in each space – much, many, lot, few or little.

1 A: How much milk do you take in your tea?
B: Just a _______, half a spoonful.

2 A: How _______ people do you know in England?
B: I know a _______ of people; from my work, my college, my neighbours, and my children's friends.

3 A: How _______ petrol does your car use?
B: It uses a _______. It's very expensive to run.

4 A: How _______ e-mails do you send every day?
B: I only send a _______, not _______; maybe two or three.

5 A: How _______ fruit do you eat every day?
B: Just a _______, not _______. I know I should eat more.

6 A: How _______ times a week do you go shopping?
B: Not _______; maybe once or twice.

5 Circle the correct option.

How much / How many sugar should I use?

a *There is a little / a few coffee left in the jar.*

b *How many / How much information do you need?*

c *There is a lot / a little of sugar in cola.*

d *Jeya has a few / a little tomatoes in her fridge.*

e *How much / How many lessons do you have on Monday?*

6 Work with a classmate. Ask and answer questions with How much and How many. Look at Exercise 2 and Exercise 4 in this unit.

For example:

A: *How much coffee do you drink?*

B: *I drink a lot – four or five cups a day.*

12 Making plurals

nouns

Database 5, 11

Use in context

There is a lot of traffic.

Read about the town centre. Look at the green words.

There are some shops in the town centre. There is a lot of traffic. We can see some cars and two buses. There are a lot of people on the streets. We can see two men with their wives and children. There is a woman wearing jeans and sunglasses.

ITALIAN DELI
There are some shops.
One of the women is wearing jeans and sunglasses.

How do we make plurals? (page 97)

Complete these examples. Some of the answers can be found in the yellow box.

1 *Most nouns + ~s:* shop → *shops*, car → _____, street → _________.

2 *Nouns ending ~s / ~sh / ~ch / ~x + ~es:* bus → ______.

3 *Nouns ending ~y change to ~ies:* baby → _______.
But for ~ay / ~ey / ~oy + ~s: boy → _____.

4 *Nouns ending ~fe change to ~ves:* wife → ________.

5 *Some nouns have special plurals:* man → _______, person → ______, child → _________.

6 *Some nouns are always plural:* jeans, s______________.

7 *Uncountable nouns are always singular:* t________.

1 Write the plurals of these nouns. If there is no plural, leave a space.

	singular	plural		singular	plural
	pen	pens	**k**	*city*	
a	*watch*		**l**	*mouse*	
b	*lady*		**m**	*sandwich*	
c	*day*		**n**	*egg*	
d	*knife*		**o**	*church*	
e	*tooth*		**p**	*week*	
f	*trousers*		**q**	*milk*	
g	*weather*		**r**	*shorts*	
h	*bag*		**s**	*camera*	
i	*bank*		**t**	*family*	
j	*box*		**u**	*gentleman*	

2 Write the singular of these nouns.

	singular	plural		singular	plural
	student	*students*	**f**		*people*
a		*women*	**g**		*loaves*
b		*houses*	**h**		*parties*
c		*dishes*	**i**		*feet*
d		*fish*	**j**		*sheep*
e		*classes*	**k**		*children*

3 Some of these sentences are right and some are wrong. Tick (✓) sentences that are right. Correct any mistakes.

She's got three ~~childs~~. children

a *The men are asking him questions.* __________

b *I can't find the keis to my house.* __________

c *I don't like English foods.* __________

d *Please put some knives and forks on the table.* __________

e *Please can you give me some informations?* __________

f *My wife gave me a new pyjama for Christmas.* __________

g *I love to eat all kinds of fish.* __________

h *There is a lot of sheep in the English countryside.* __________

i *There are twelve persons in my class.* __________

4 Look at the pictures and circle the correct plural form to complete the phrases.

Some bread / breads. Three loafs / loaves of bread / breads.

a *Some milk / milks. Two bottle / bottles of milk / milks.*

b *Some eggs / egges. A dozen / A dozen of eggs / egges.*

c *A pyjama / Some pyjamas. Two / A pair of pyjama / pyjamas.*

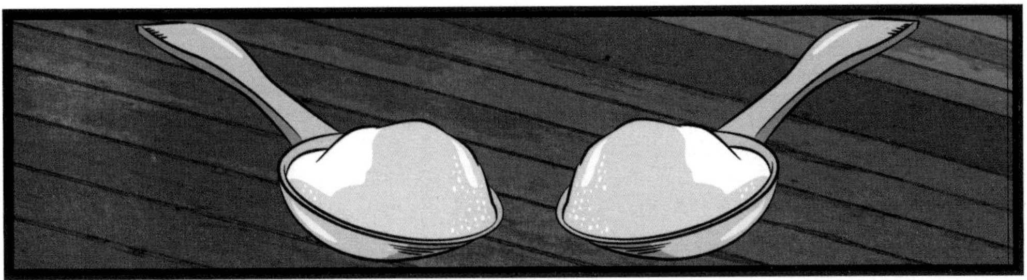

d *Some sugar / sugars. Two spoonsful / spoonfuls of sugar / sugars.*

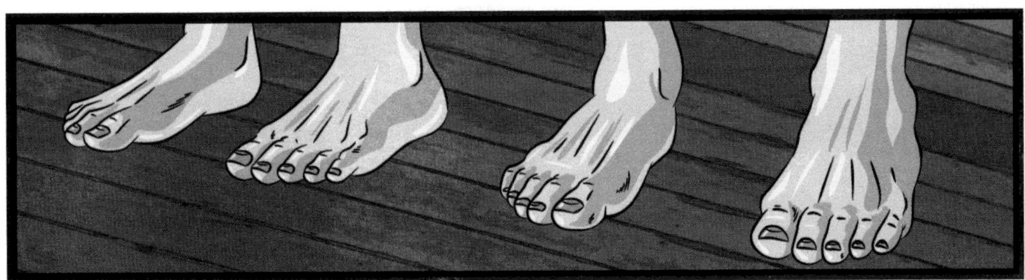

e *Some feet / feets. Two / Two pairs of feet / feets.*

f *Some persons / people. A group of / Groups of people / peoples.*

5 **Work with a classmate. Think of ten nouns and then ask your partner to write the plurals.**

13 a / an / the

articles

Database 4, 14

Use in context

Jasmeena

The university is in the countryside.

Read about where these people live and work. Look at the green words.

Cheng is a student at City College. He lives in a flat. The flat is near the college.

Jasmeena is a university teacher. She works at Sussex University. The university is in the countryside.

Ismail is an engineer. He works in an office. The office is in the city centre. It takes an hour and ten minutes to get to work.

When do we use a / an / the? (page 98)

Complete the examples.

1. ***We use a before a noun. The noun is not special:*** *a student, _____ flat.*
2. ***We use an before <u>a, e, i, o, u</u>:*** *_____ engineer, _______ office.*
3. ***We use an before a silent <u>h</u>:*** *_______________ and ten minutes.*
4. ***We use a before <u>u</u> pronounced /juː/:*** *_______________ teacher.*
5. ***We use the when the noun is special or we know the person, place or thing:***
__________ flat is near ________ college. ______________________________ is in _________________________. ______________________ is in ____________________ centre.

Practice

1 Write a or an.

a bus

a ____ lesson	**b** ____ egg	**c** ____ university	**d** ____ son
e ____ apple	**f** ____ bottle	**g** ____ umbrella	**h** ____ computer
i ____ hour	**j** ____ hospital	**k** ____ insect	**l** ____ woman
m ____ European city	**n** ____ old car	**o** ____ orange room	**p** ____ new book
q ____ question	**r** ____ house	**s** ____ actor	

2 Correct the mistakes in these sentences.

A dog is a animal. an animal

a *Pawel works as a electrician.* ____________________

b *A food at Mario's restaurant is very good.* ____________________

c *The train is a hour late.* ____________________

d *Excuse me, can you tell me a time?* ____________________

e *Aisha works at an University Hospital. She is the nurse.* ____________________ ____________________

f *Hamid lives in an nice house. An house has three bedrooms and the garden.*
____________________ ____________________ ____________________

g *I want to see a new film at a cinema.* ____________________ ____________________

3 Match the two parts of each sentence. Write a, an or the in each space.

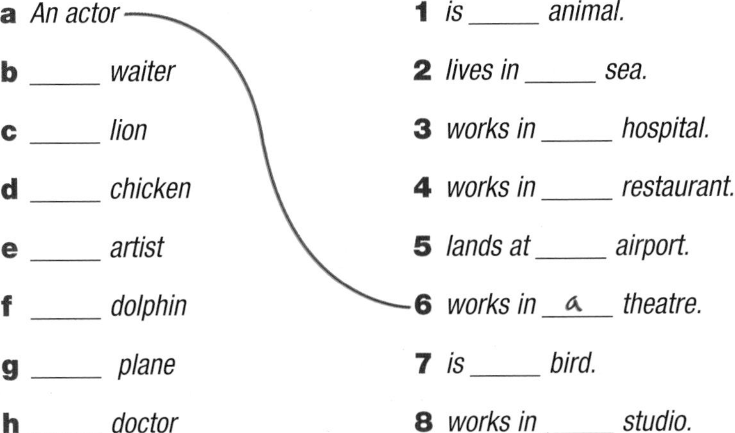

a *An actor*	**1** *is _____ animal.*
b _____ *waiter*	**2** *lives in _____ sea.*
c _____ *lion*	**3** *works in _____ hospital.*
d _____ *chicken*	**4** *works in _____ restaurant.*
e _____ *artist*	**5** *lands at _____ airport.*
f _____ *dolphin*	**6** *works in* a *theatre.*
g _____ *plane*	**7** *is _____ bird.*
h _____ *doctor*	**8** *works in _____ studio.*

4 **Jeya and Deva are in a snack bar. Complete the conversation with a, an or the.**

Assistant: *What are you going to have?*

Jeya: *I'll have ______ sandwich, please. ______ egg sandwich.*

Deva: *And I'll have _____ piece of cake and ______ apple.*

Assistant: *Which cake would you like?*

Deva: *______ chocolate cake, I think.*

Assistant: *And would you like _____ drink?*

Jeya: *_____ cup of black coffee for me.*

Deva: *And just _____ orange juice for me, please.*

Assistant: *Where are you sitting?*

Jeya: *At _____ table in _____ window, by _____ door.*

Assistant: *OK, I'll bring __________ sandwich over to you when it's ready.*

5 **Work with a classmate. Write down ten nouns. Ask your partner to tell you if we use a, an or the.**

4

the

the definite article

Database 3, 6

Hamid
I come from Islamabad in Pakistan.

When do we use the?

(page 98)

A Put the correct words in the spaces.

stations and airports	~~streets and roads~~
schools and colleges	countries
towns and cities	college subjects

We don't usually use the before:

: 35 Hurst Road

__________________: Islamabad, Crawley

__________________: Pakistan, England

__________________: Gatwick Airport

__________________: Central Sussex College

__________________: English

There are a few exceptions to these rules (see page 98): for example, the United Kingdom.

Hamid is talking about where he lives. Look at the green words.

"I come from Islamabad in Pakistan but now I live in England. My address is 35 Hurst Road, Crawley, not far from Gatwick Airport. I study English at Central Sussex College. I like living in the United Kingdom."

Now read what Hamid says about food. Look at the green words.

"I don't eat meat. I like fish and I have a lot of fruit and vegetables. I don't think the food in England is very good. The children here eat a lot of salt, fat and sugar."

B Complete the examples.

1 ***We don't usually use the when we talk about things or people generally:*** meat, f____t, v__________, s________, f________, s________.

2 ***We use the when we talk about specific things or people:*** the food in England, __________________ here.

Practice

1 **Write the if necessary.**

______ *North Street*	*The United Kingdom*	
a ______ *Birmingham*	**f** ______ *River Nile*	**k** ______ *European Union*
b ______ *mathematics*	**g** ______ *Paris*	**l** ______ *Heathrow Airport*
c ______ *Victoria Station*	**h** ______ *Buckingham Road*	**m** ______ *United Arab Emirates*
d ______ *United States*	**i** ______ *Asia*	**n** ______ *London City University*
e ______ *India*	**j** ______ *business studies*	

2 **Write these sentences in the correct order.**

sun / The / shining / is The sun is shining.

a *The / interesting / talk / was*

b *road / car / the / The / drove / up*

c *flowers / beautiful / The / were*

d *I / window / by / the / sat*

e *ate / She / cake / the*

3 **Write the if necessary.**

a *I love ____ hamburgers.*

b *Can you turn off* the *television, please?*

c *He doesn't drink ______ wine.*

d *What do you usually have for ____ breakfast?*

e *______ breakfast in our hotel is fantastic.*

f *I like taking ______ photos.*

g *______ photos of your wedding are really good.*

h *My favourite hobby is ______ shopping.*

i *I don't like ______ sport.*

j *_______ weather in Yorkshire is wonderful.*

k *I am studying _______ history.*

l *I'm very interested in ______ history of my town.*

4 Write about yourself.

I come from (a) ______________ *in* (b) ______________ *but now I live in* (c) ______________.
My address is (d) ______________ *in* (e) ______________. *My nearest station is* (f) ______________.
My nearest airport is (g) ______________. *I study* (h) ____________ *at* (i) ______________. *I work as a* (j) ____________ *in* (k) ______________. *I would like to visit* (l) ______________.

5 Now work with a classmate. Ask and answer questions about your answers to Exercise 4.

For example:

A: *What city do you come from?*

B: *I come from Krackow in Poland.*

6 Work with a classmate. You should each choose one general subject from A and talk about it for 30 seconds. Then talk about a special subject from B.

A	*B*
shopping	*the weather at the moment*
football	*the latest news*
smoking	*the places to go in town*
work	*the local trains and buses*
holidays	*the class you are in*

15 this / that / these / those

demonstratives

Database 12

Use in context

Jasmeena

Jasmeena is showing Ling some family photographs. Look at the green words.

Ling: *Who's **this**?*
Jasmeena: ***This** is my mother and **these** are my two sisters.*
Ling: *And what about that old photo over there? Who's **that**?*
Jasmeena: *Oh, **those** two people are my grandparents, and **that** young girl is my mother!*

... these are my two sisters.

When do we use this / that / these / those?

(page 98)

Complete the sentences using this, that, these or those.

1 *For things and people near to us, we use* this *for one thing or person and* __________ *for two or more things or people.*

2 *For things and people not very near to us, we use* _______ *for one thing or person and* __________ *for two or more things or people.*

Practice

1 Circle the correct option.

Please give me (that) / those plate.

a *Can you move this / these chair for me, please?*

b *Whose are that / those glasses?*

c *Do you like this / these jeans?*

d *What's the name of this / these vegetable?*

e *This / These is my friend Ibrahim.*

f *A: Hello, who's that / those?*
B: This / These is Petra here. May I speak to Jan?

g *I'd like one of that / those cakes, please.*

h *This / These fish isn't fresh.*

i *I like this / that car over there on the other side of the road.*

2 Surinder works with old people in a care home. Write the correct word: this / that / these / those.

Can you help me with this *coat?*

a *Are ____________ your glasses?*

b *Can you get me ____________ stick?*

c *Would you like some of ____________ soup?*

d *Aren't ____________ flowers lovely?*

e *You need to take ____________ medicine.*

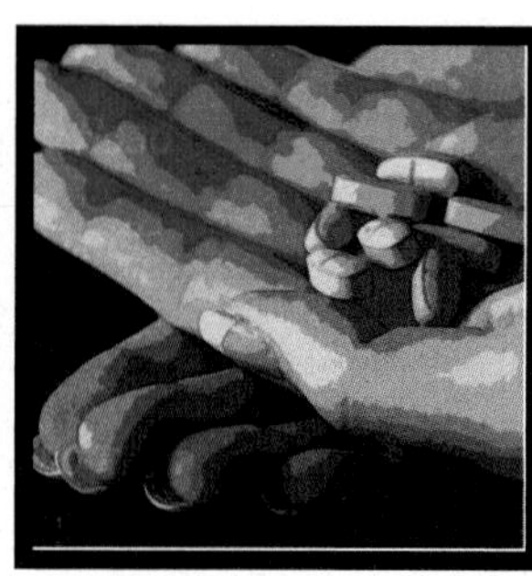

f *It's time for you to take ____________ pills.*

g *Can you get me ____________ suitcase?*

3 Write the best word – this, that, these or those – in each sentence.

I think this *is the best day of my life!*

a *Hello, Mikel. _______ is Said, my brother.*

b *Which picture do you prefer – _________ one here or __________ one there?*

c *Do you know _________ new student sitting by the window?*

d *I can't find ______ keys Obi gave me.*

e *A: Thanks for your help.*
B: ______'s OK, no problem.

f *I'd like one of _________ large screen televisions but I haven't got enough money.*

g *Please fill in ______ form here with your name, address and details.*

h *_______ pen doesn't work. Look, there's no ink in it.*

i *Here you are. Can you post ________ letters for me, please?*

4 Quiz. Work with a partner. Think of ten things (or people!) you have with you, near you and around the room to practise this, that, these and those. Show or point to the things and ask your partner to name them. (Make sure you use this and these for things that are near to you and your partner!)

For example:

A: *What's this?*

B: *This is a watch.*

A: *And those are …?*

B: *Those are tables.*

6 Pronouns

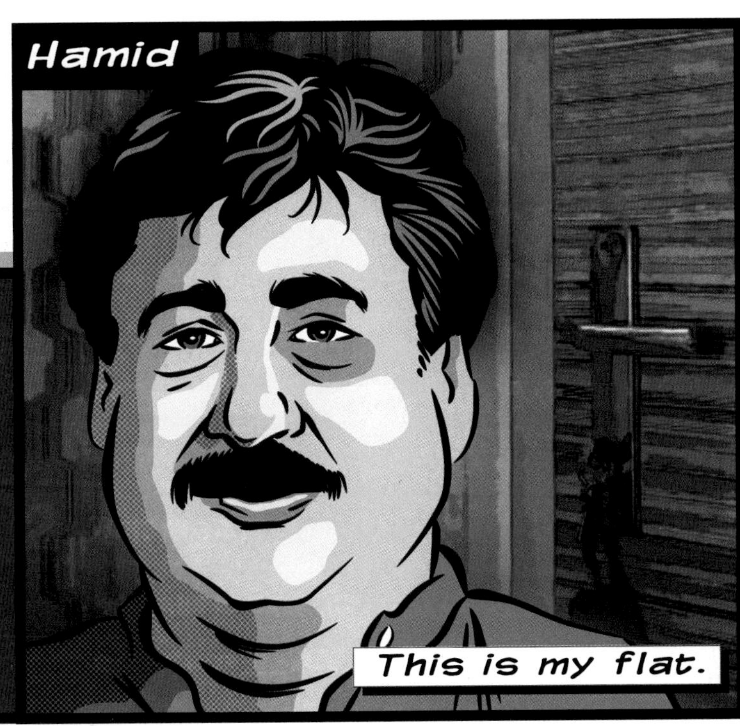

Rafiq and Hamid are looking at photographs of where they live. Read the conversation and look at the green words.

Rafiq: Have **you** got a flat?
Hamid: Yes, this is **my** flat.
Rafiq: Is it rented or is it **your** flat?
Hamid: It's **mine**. It belongs to **me**. What about you?
Rafiq: I live with **my** wife. **We**'ve got a house. It belongs to **us**. **My** wife likes gardening. Look, this is **her** garden.

How do we use personal pronouns? (page 98)

Complete the table with the correct pronouns.

Subject	Object	Possessive	
I've got a flat.	It belongs to __me__.	It's ______ flat.	It's ______.
______'ve got a flat.	It belongs to you.	It's ______ flat.	It's yours.
He's got a flat.	It belongs to him.	It's ______ flat.	It's his.
She's got a garden.	It belongs to her.	It's ______ garden.	It's hers.
______'ve got a house.	It belongs to ______.	It's our house.	It's ours.
They've got a house.	It belongs to them.	It's their house.	It's ______.

Practice

1 **Write the correct word: I, you, he, she, we or they.**

Excuse me, can you *tell me the time, please?*

a *Mikel is my husband. ______ is 28 years old.*

b *I love my mother. _____ is my best friend.*

c *I'm sorry but ____ can't help you.*

d *I live with Saeed. ____ are brothers.*

e *I like my neighbours. _________ are very friendly.*

2 **Write the correct word: me, you, him, her, us or them.**

This is my car. It belongs to me.

a *My parents are in India. I miss __________.*

b *Deva isn't happy with Rafiq. She's angry with _________.*

c *Hello, we need a taxi, please. Can you pick _______ up at 6.30?*

d *Your daughter is crying. You need to talk to ________.*

3 **Write the correct word: my, your, his, her, our or their.**

I want to call Mr Jackson. Have you got his *number?*

a *Excuse me, can I see ______ passport, please?*

b *She's happy because she's meeting _____ friends tonight.*

c *My son is very happy at _____ school.*

d *The parents pick up _______ children from school every day.*

4 **Write the correct word: mine, yours, his, hers, ours or theirs.**

That car belongs to my brother. I know that it's his.

a *This is my sister's mobile phone. I'm sure it is ________.*

b *A: Whose is this bag? Is it ________? B: No, it isn't ________.*

c *A: Does that house belong to your family? B: Yes, it's __________.*

d *I'm giving my address to everyone in the class and they are all giving me _________.*

5 Circle the correct option.

She / Her car is yellow.

a *Please tell me / my you / your name.*

b *His / Him sister is in me / my class.*

c *That's hers / her jacket and this is my / mine.*

d *Please come and visit we / us in ours / our country.*

e *Us / Our neighbours are on holiday with them / their children.*

6 Work in a group. One student collects two objects from the others in the group. The first student then asks the others questions with pronouns.

A: *Is this your mobile phone?*

B: *No, it isn't mine.*

A: *Is it his?*

B: *Yes, it belongs to him.*

17 Adjectives

Database 2

Use in context

Roman

Read the description of Roman. Look at the words in green.

This is Roman. He is tall and good-looking. Roman is wearing a white T-shirt, blue jeans and a pair of old trainers. He's got a new mobile phone in his hand. He looks happy. He feels good.

He looks happy.

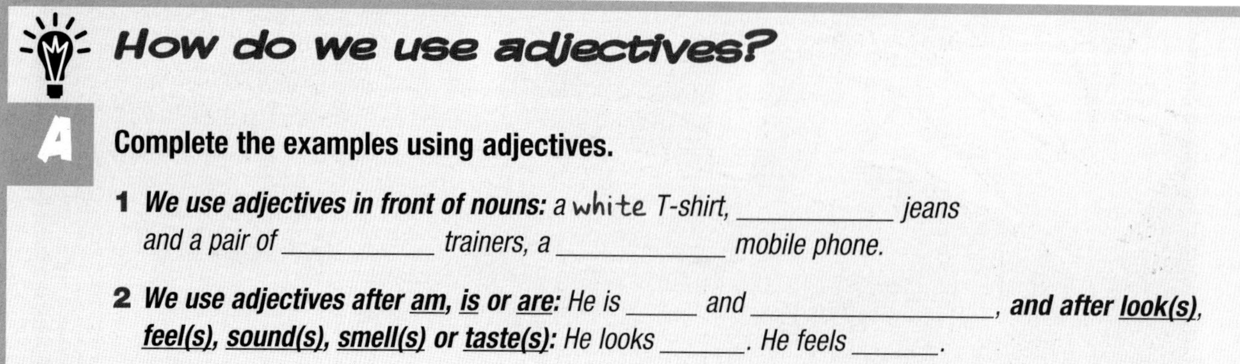

How do we use adjectives?

A **Complete the examples using adjectives.**

1 ***We use adjectives in front of nouns:*** *a* white *T-shirt, ___________ jeans and a pair of ___________ trainers, a ___________ mobile phone.*

2 ***We use adjectives after <u>am</u>, <u>is</u> or <u>are</u>:*** *He is _____ and _______________,* ***and after <u>look(s)</u>, <u>feel(s)</u>, <u>sound(s)</u>, <u>smell(s)</u> or <u>taste(s)</u>:*** *He looks ______. He feels ______.*

Practice

1 **Put the words in the correct order to make sentences.**

an / man / is / He / old He is an old man.

a *got / shoes / new / some / I've*

b *These / eggs / fresh / are*

c *wearing / She / is / jeans / blue*

d *youngest / is / my / This / daughter*

e *There / black / in / are / clouds / sky / the*

2 **Write these sentences in the correct order.**

tall / is / He He is tall.

a *fine / weather / The / is*

b *feels / cold / room / This*

c *not / am / happy / I*

d *She / hungry / feel / doesn't*

e *job / interesting / sounds / The*

3 **These sentences are wrong. Correct the mistakes.**

He's wearing a ~~shirt blue~~. a blue shirt

a *I give money to people poor.* ______________________________

b *Look at the beautifuls flowers.* ______________________________

c *The student very young looks.* ______________________________

d *Very hungry I am.* ______________________________

e *She isn't feeling happily today.* ______________________________

4 Look at the pictures. Choose words from the box to make sentences.

~~is~~	*looks*	*smell*	*tastes*	*sounds*	*feels*	*lovely*	*terrible*
		~~hungry~~	*exciting*	*beautiful*	*sad*		

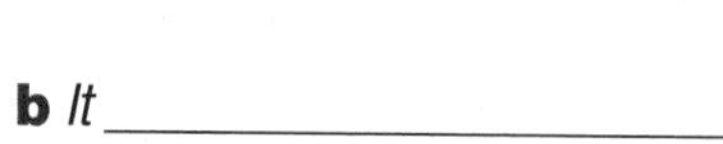

a *She* is hungry. **b** *It* ________________ **c** *He* ________________

d *They* ________________ **e** *Your news* ________________ **f** *She* ________________

5 Work with a classmate. Choose someone in the class to describe to your partner. Describe them using adjectives. Can your partner say who it is?

For example:

A: *She is tall. She's got long, brown hair. She's wearing a red sweater, a white shirt and blue jeans.*

B: *I think it's Kamila.*

8 Adverbs

Use in context

Cheng

How is your English, Cheng?

Cheng is talking to his teacher. Read the conversation and look at the green words.

Teacher: *How is your English, Cheng?*
Cheng: *OK, I think. It's not bad. I can understand easily when people speak English clearly. I can't understand well if they speak fast. My big problem is reading and writing. I read slowly and I write badly. I'm working hard to get better.*

How do we use adverbs? (page 98–99)

1 ***We use adverbs after most verbs – understand*** *easily (~~understand easy~~),* ***speak English*** *clearly (~~speak clear~~, ~~speak clearly English~~).*

2 ***We do not use adverbs after am, is or are (or feel, look, sound, taste, smell) – it's not*** *bad (~~it's not well~~).*

Complete the examples.

1 ***Regular adverbs add ~ly to the adjective:*** *clear –* clearly, *slow –* ____________, *bad –* ____________.
Regular adverbs ending in ~y change ~y to ~ily: *easy –* ____________.

2 ***Irregular adverbs include:*** *good –* ____________, *fast –* ____________, *hard –* ____________.

1 Write the adverbs for these adjectives.

clear clearly

a *slow* ______________________

b *quick* ______________________

c *happy* ______________________

d *careful* ______________________

e *quiet* ______________________

f *angry* ______________________

g *fast* ______________________

h *bad* ______________________

i *good* ______________________

j *hard* ______________________

k *heavy* ______________________

l *dangerous* ______________________

m *serious* ______________________

n *safe* ______________________

o *strong* ______________________

2 Some of these sentences are correct and some are wrong. Tick (✔) the ones that are right and correct the mistakes.

Magda speaks English ~~good~~. Magda speaks English well.

a *Jeya walks quickly.* ______________________

b *I can't understand. Please speak slow.* ______________________

c *I usually sleep well.* ______________________

d *Don't drive fast in the city centre.* ______________________

e *Cheng works hardly at his English.* ______________________

f *Petra laughs happy.* ______________________

g *Please talk quietly in the library.* ______________________

h *Hamid very well plays tennis.* ______________________

i *Rafiq drives very carefully.* ______________________

3 Choose words from the box to make sentences about yourself.

well	*badly*	*easily*	*fast*	*hard*	*quickly*	*slowly*	*safely*
carefully	*strongly*	*dangerously*	*seriously*				

I speak English — I speak English slowly and carefully.

a *I read English* ______________________

b *I write in English* ______________________

c *I drive* ______________________

d *I cook* ______________________

e *I can swim* ______________________

f *I play tennis* ______________________

g *I ride a bicycle* ______________________

h *I work* ______________________

i *I study* ______________________

4 Work with a classmate. Ask and answer questions about Exercise 3 above. You can ask questions with *How do you ...?* or with *Can you ...?*

For example:

A: *How do you drive?* **B:** *I drive well. I drive slowly and carefully.*

A: *Can you cook?* **B:** *No, I cook very badly.*

5 Match the two parts of each sentence.

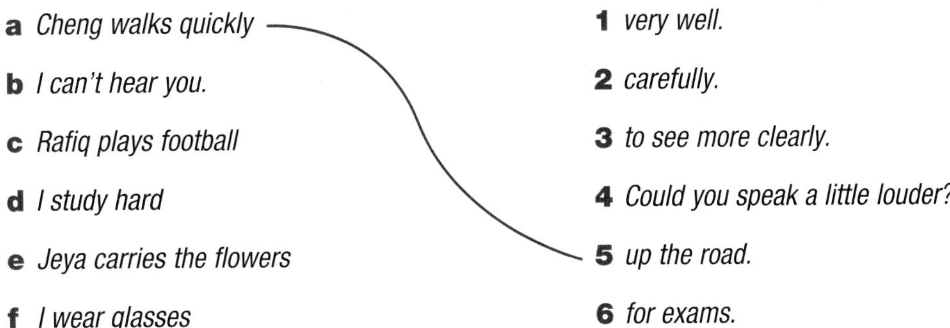

a *Cheng walks quickly*
b *I can't hear you.*
c *Rafiq plays football*
d *I study hard*
e *Jeya carries the flowers*
f *I wear glasses*

1 *very well.*
2 *carefully.*
3 *to see more clearly.*
4 *Could you speak a little louder?*
5 *up the road.*
6 *for exams.*

19 Prepositions of time

in / on / at

Database 16

Use in context

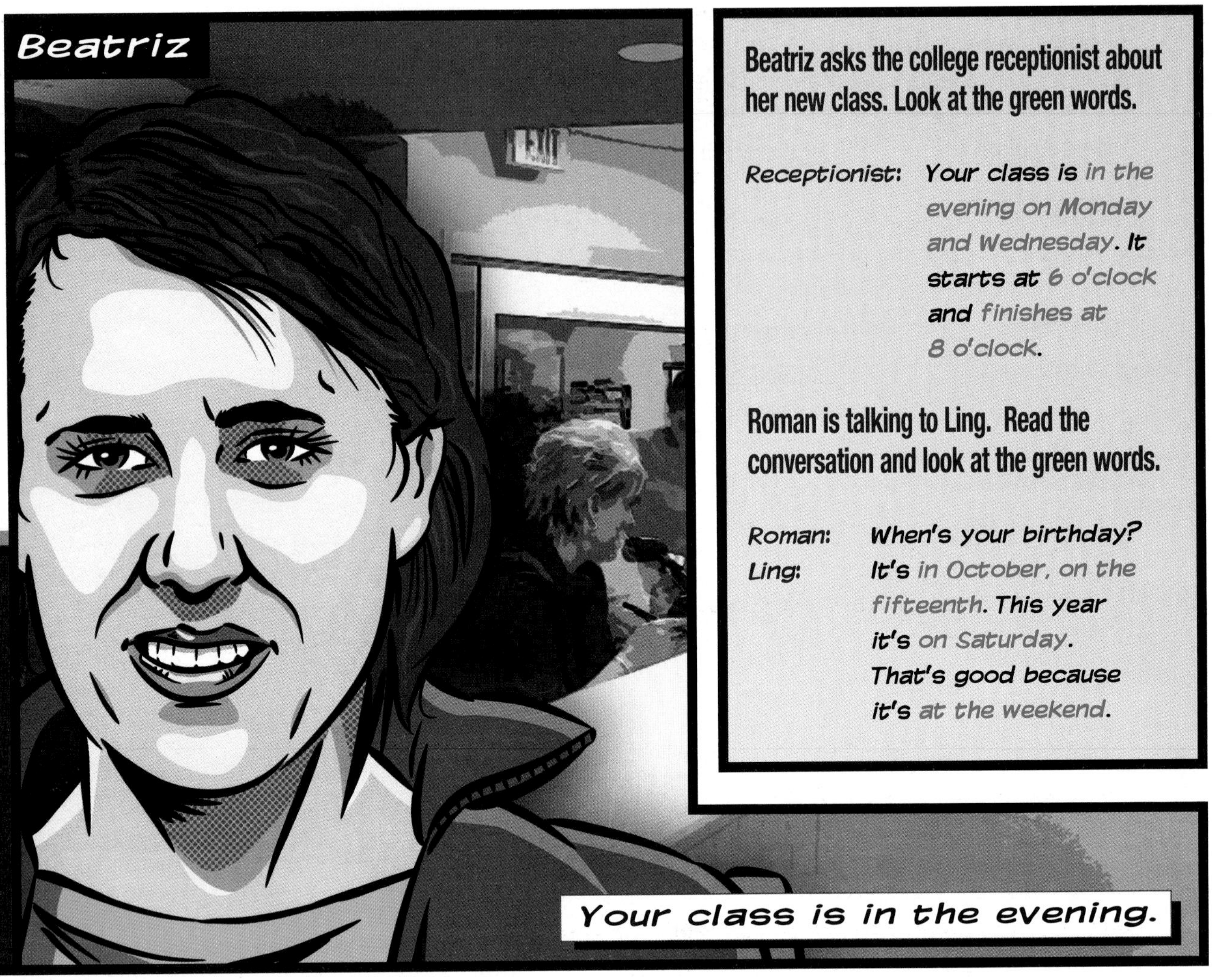

Beatriz

Beatriz asks the college receptionist about her new class. Look at the green words.

Receptionist: Your class is in the evening on Monday and Wednesday. It starts at 6 o'clock and finishes at 8 o'clock.

Roman is talking to Ling. Read the conversation and look at the green words.

Roman: When's your birthday?
Ling: It's in October, on the fifteenth. This year it's on Saturday. That's good because it's at the weekend.

Your class is in the evening.

How do we use in, on and at for times?

(page 99)

A **Write in, on or at in the examples.**

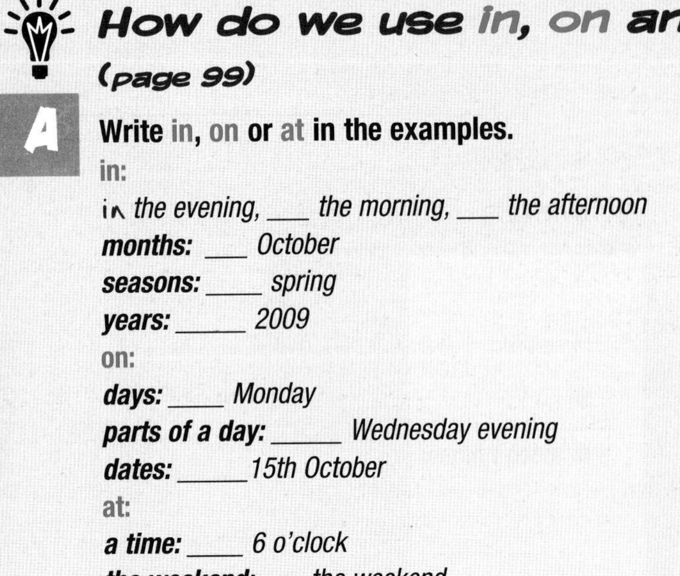

in:
in the evening, ___ the morning, ___ the afternoon
months: ___ October
seasons: ___ spring
years: ___ 2009
on:
days: ___ Monday
parts of a day: ___ Wednesday evening
dates: ___ 15th October
at:
a time: ___ 6 o'clock
the weekend: ___ the weekend
night: ___ night

Practice

1 **Circle the correct option.**

in / (on) / at Friday

a *in /on / at Thursday*
b *in / on / at July*
c *in / on / at Saturday morning*
d *in / on / at 1995*
e *in / on / at the weekend*
f *in / on / at winter*
g *in / on / at one o'clock*
h *in / on / at the afternoon*
i *in / on / at summer*
j *in / on / at 23rd January*
k *in / on / at night*
l *in / on / at a quarter past five*
m *in / on / at Sunday night*
n *in / on / at 25th May*

2 **Write in, on or at.**

We always go out on Saturday night.

a *I start work ___ 8.00 and I finish ___ 5.30.*

b *I don't usually work ___ the weekend, but I work ___ Saturday mornings when we are very busy.*

c *He has two weeks' holiday ___ August.*

d *She picks the children up from school ___ half past three.*

e *Their wedding is ___ Saturday 5th July.*

3 **Look at Ling's diary. Then write in, on or at to complete the sentences on the next page.**

Monday 6.00 p.m. College	*Thursday* 8.00 a.m. Work at supermarket 7.30 p.m. Film at Multiplex
Tuesday 8.00 a.m. Work at supermarket	*Friday* 8.00 p.m. Meal at the China Garden
Wednesday 6.00 p.m. College	*Saturday* 3.00 p.m. Naomi's wedding Evening - wedding party
	Sunday 11.00 a.m. Meet Shu in London

a *Ling goes to college* on *Monday and Wednesday ___ 6 o'clock ___ the evening.*

b *She goes to work ___ 8 o'clock ___ the morning ___ Tuesday and Thursday.*

c *___ Thursday ___ half past seven ___ the evening she's going to see a film.*

d *She's having a meal at the China Garden ___ Friday ___ 8 o'clock ___ the evening.*

e *___ Saturday, she's going to a wedding ___ three ___ the afternoon. Then there's a wedding party ___ Saturday evening.*

f *___ Sunday, she's meeting Shu ___ eleven ___ the morning in London.*

4 Write a diary for next week. Write something for each day. Then work with a classmate. Ask and answer questions about different times and days.

For example:

A: *What are you doing on Monday?*

B: *I start work at 8 o'clock and finish at 1 o'clock. I'm coming to college at 5.30 in the evening.*

Monday	*Thursday*
Tuesday	*Friday*
Wednesday	*Saturday*
	Sunday

Prepositions of place

in / on / at

Database 17

Ismail
This morning he is in his car.

Read about Ismail, Magda and Hamid. Look at the green words.

Ismail lives in Birmingham, in the Midlands. He works in an office in the city centre. This morning he is in his car. Magda lives in Lincoln Street, in Brighton, on the south coast. She is a teacher at Sussex University. She is waiting at the bus stop. Hamid lives at 35 Hurst Road, in Crawley. He works at Gatwick Airport. He lives in a flat on the first floor. At the moment he's on the bus.

How do we use in, on and at for places?

(page 99)

A **Write in, on or at to complete the examples.**

***In* is used for the following:**
Streets, towns and areas: in *Birmingham,* ____ *the city centre,* ____ *Brighton,* ____ *Lincoln Street,* ____ *Crawley*
Regions: ____ *the Midlands*
Houses, flats, rooms: ____ *a flat,* ____ *an office*
Cars, taxis: ____ *his car.*
***On* is used for the following:**
The coast: ____ *the south coast*
Floors: ____ *the first floor*
Buses, trains, planes, boats: ____ *the bus*
***At* is used for the following:**
Places of work and study: ____ *Sussex University,* ____ *Gatwick Airport*
Next to a point: ____ *the bus stop*
Addresses: ____ *35 Hurst Road*

Practice

1 Match the two parts of each sentence.

a	*She's reading in*	**1**	*12 Church Road.*
b	*He lives in*	**2**	*the traffic lights.*
c	*He works at*	**3**	*the library.*
d	*They study at*	**4**	*the third floor.*
e	*She lives on*	**5**	*the bus.*
f	*I live at*	**6**	*the local hospital.*
g	*The car is waiting at*	**7**	*London.*
h	*She's travelling on*	**8**	*Oxford University.*

2 Circle the correct option. Choose in, on or at.

He's in / on / at the bathroom.

a *She's in / on / at the kitchen.*

b *They live in / on / at Manchester.*

c *He's in / on / at a taxi.*

d *The office is in / on / at the second floor.*

e *I'm meeting her in / on / at Victoria Station.*

f *She lives in / on / at the north of England.*

g *New York is in / on / at the East Coast.*

h *I live in / on / at 97 South Street.*

i *They study in / on / at the college.*

3 Write in, on or at to complete these sentences.

Ling lives in a flat.

a *The flat is _______ the ground floor.*

b *She lives _______ Church Road.*

c *Ling lives _______ Crawley, _______ West Sussex.*

d *She studies English _______ the local college.*

e *The class is ________ the third floor.*

f *She works part-time _______ the supermarket.*

4 Write about where you live, work and study.

house? flat? room? I live in two rooms in a big house.

a *floor?* ____

b *street?* ____

c *number?* ____

d *town? city? county? region?* ____

e *college?* ____

f *classroom?* ____

g *workplace?* ____

5 Work with a classmate. Ask and answer questions about the places where you live, work and study. Also ask about friends and family.

For example:

A: *Do you live in a house or a flat?*

B: *In a flat.*

A: *Which floor is it on?*

B: *It's on the first floor.*

More prepositions of place

Database 10

Look at the town plan and read the sentences. Look at the green words.

The bank is next to the supermarket. The road goes under the bridge. There is a cash machine in front of the bank. The doctor's surgery is behind the supermarket. The post office is opposite or facing the lake. The chemist's is between the post office and the café. The post office is on the right. The café is on the left, and the chemist's is in the middle. The park is near the supermarket, by the doctor's surgery.

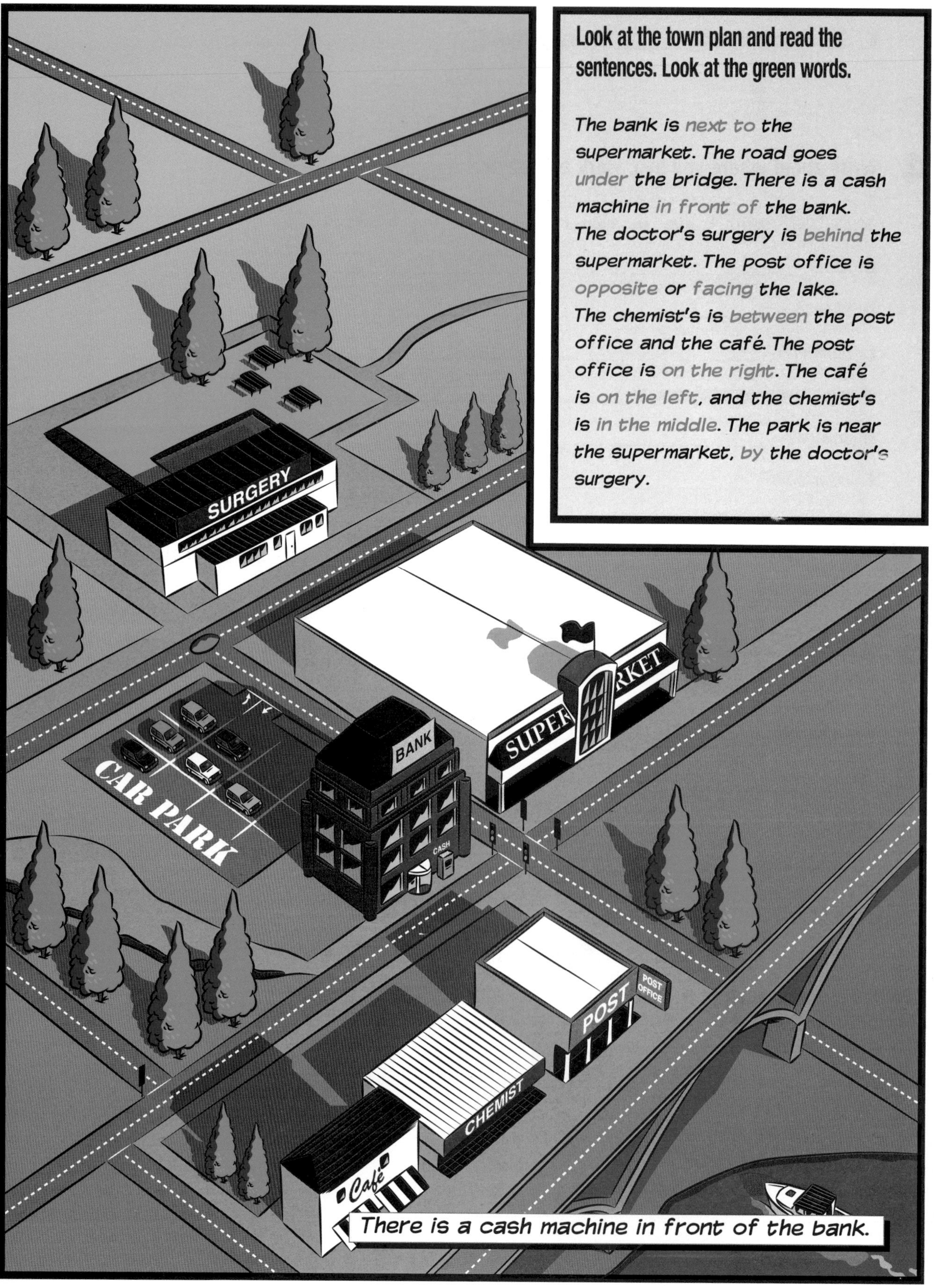

There is a cash machine in front of the bank.

Use in context

1 Look at the town plan on the previous page. Answer the questions correctly.

Is the bank facing the supermarket? No, it isn't. It's next to the supermarket.

a *Is the park near the supermarket?* ____________________

b *Is the post office next to the chemist's?* ____________________

c *Does the road go under the supermarket?* ____________________

d *Is there a cash machine in front of the post office?* ____________________

e *Is the café by the park?* ____________________

f *Is the chemist's between the café and the post office?* ____________________

g *Is the post office on the left of the chemist's?* ____________________

h *Is the bank behind the post office?* ____________________

i *Is the doctor's surgery in front of the supermarket?* ____________________

j *Is the car park behind the chemist's?* ____________________

2 Work with a classmate. Look at the town plan again for 30 seconds. Cover the plan and ask and answer these questions. Don't look!

a *Excuse me, where's the car park, please?*

b *Excuse me, where's the doctor's surgery, please?*

c *Excuse me, where's there a chemist's, please?*

d *Excuse me, is there a cash machine near here, please?*

e *And where is the bank?*

f *Excuse me, is there a café in the town?*

g *Excuse me, can you tell me where the post office is, please?*

h *Excuse me, is there a park near here, please?*

3 Where are these things in Ismail's office? Write one word on each line.

The window is behind *Ismail's desk.*

a *Ismail's desk is* _____ __________ _____ *the window.*

b *His chair is* __________ *his desk.*

c *The paper is* ____________ *his desk.*

d *His files are* __________ *the window,* _______ _______ *left.*

e *The photocopier is* _________ *Ismail's desk,* ______ ______ __________.

f *His desk is* _______ _______ ___________ *of the room,* __________ *the door and the photocopier.*

g *There are two chairs* __________ *his desk.*

4 Think of your kitchen. Quickly draw the room and the things in it. Show your partner your drawing and ask and answer questions. Then do the same for other rooms and for your workplace.

For example:

A: *Where's the washing machine?*

B: *It's under the window next to the sink.*

Prepositional phrases

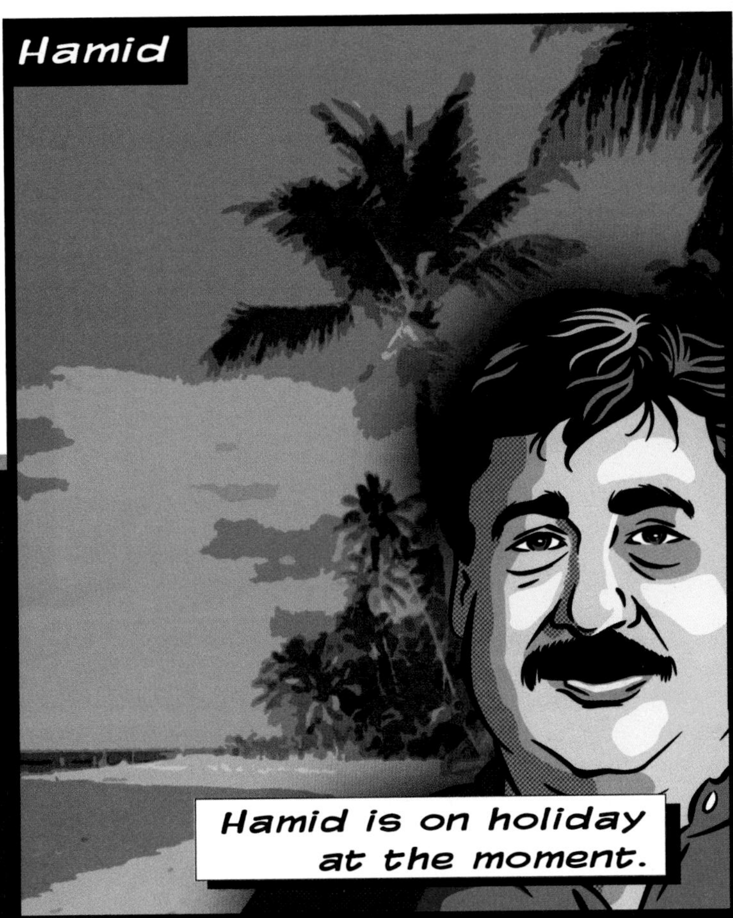
Hamid
Hamid is on holiday at the moment.

Read about Ismail, Magda and Hamid. Look at the green words.

Ismail goes to work by car. He gets to work at 8.30. He's always on time. He spends the first hour at work on the phone or on the computer answering e-mails. Sometimes, he travels on business. In the evening, he usually gets home at about 6.00. He goes to bed at about 11.00.

Magda goes to work by bus, or sometimes on foot if the weather is nice. She gets on the bus at the stop near her flat. Sometimes she works at home. In the evening, she usually reads in bed if there is nothing on the television or on the radio.

Hamid is on holiday at the moment.

How do we use prepositional phrases?

(page 99)

A **Complete these examples.**

to:
He goes to work (~~the~~ work). He gets _____ work. He goes _____ bed (~~the~~ bed).
on:
He's always _____ time. He is _____ the phone. He travels ____ business. She goes to work ___ foot.
She gets _____ the bus. She is _____ holiday. There is nothing _____ the television.
by:
He goes to work _____ car (~~the~~ car). She goes to work _____ bus.
at:
He is _____ work (~~the~~ work). She works _____ home (~~the~~ home).
in:
She reads ____ bed (~~the~~ bed)
No preposition:
He usually gets home late.

Practice

1 Match the two parts of each sentence.

a *He's working on* — **3** *the computer at the moment.*

b *He's at*

c *She's sitting on*

d *They always go on*

e *She reads in*

f *She never stays at*

g *Sorry, she's talking on*

h *I like travelling by*

1 *bed every night.*

2 *train.*

3 *the computer at the moment.*

4 *the phone at the moment.*

5 *home at the weekend.*

6 *holiday in July.*

7 *work today.*

8 *the bus with her friend.*

2 Circle the correct option.

She goes to home / goes home at 5.30.

a *She gets to home / gets home at 6.00.*

b *I go to work / go work every day.*

c *I get to work / get work at 9.00.*

d *He normally works home / works at home.*

e *They usually go to the bed / go to bed early.*

f *I get on the train / get on train at Victoria Station.*

g *In London I travel by the bus / by bus.*

3 Choose one preposition from the box to complete the sentences. One sentence has no preposition.

~~on~~ on on in at by

He is in New York on *business at the moment.*

a *I don't enjoy travelling ___ plane.*

b *We normally cook ___ home.*

c *I never get ___ home before 8.00 in the evening.*

d *Please come to the lessons ___ time.*

e *I am always ___ bed before midnight.*

f *I'm ___ the bus at the moment.*

4 Work with a classmate. Ask and answer questions using prepositional phrases. Ask about going to work, getting home, being at home, travelling, television or holidays.

For example:

A: *How do you get to work?*

B: *I get to work by bus.*

23 Verbs + prepositions

Database 17

Myra
Hurry up and put on your coat!

It's breakfast time and Myra is talking to her son. Look at the green words.

Myra: Ali, turn off your PlayStation and listen to me! I'll pick you up from school at 3.30 today. Wait for me if I'm late. Come on now, hurry up and put on your coat!

Jasmeena works in a care home. She looks after old people. Read her conversation with one of her patients and look at the green words.

Jasmeena: Would you like to look at a magazine, Mrs Green? I'll put it on the table.

Mrs Green: Thank you, Jasmeena. I can't find my handbag.

Jasmeena: Don't worry, I'll look for it.

Use in context

How do we use verbs + prepositions?

(page 99–100)

A **Complete these examples.**

to:
listen to me, belong ____ me, write ____ me,
talk ____ me, speak ____ me
for:
wait ____ me, ask someone ____ something, thank someone ____ something
up:
pick someone ____ (collect), hurry ____, get ____ (out of bed), clean ____, tidy ____,
wash ____ (dishes)
on:
come ____ (hurry up), go ____ (continue), depend ____ someone
on/off:
switch ____ / off, turn ____ / off, put ____ / off, take ____ / off (clothes)
Some verbs + prepositions have different meanings:
look ________ = take care of, look ________ = read, look ________ = try to find

Practice

1 Circle the correct option.

My husband never listens at / on / (to) *me.*

a *This house doesn't belong* at / on / to *me.*

b *I'm going into this shop. Please wait* by / for / on *me here.*

c *Amir doesn't talk* at / to / for *his wife.*

d *Please hurry* up / down / after *or we'll be late.*

e *He puts* off / on / down *a clean shirt every day.*

f *Don't forget to turn* off / on / in *the television before you go to bed.*

g *What time do you want me to pick you* for / down / up *this evening?*

h *I work as a carer looking* at / for / after *disabled people.*

2 Choose the correct verb from the box.

writes	belongs	~~thanks~~	depends	washes	takes	tidies	turns

She always thanks *me for helping her.*

a *He never* ______ *up after a meal.*

b *This switch* ______ *off all the electricity.*

c *She* _____ *to her parents every week.*

d *We could have a picnic but it* _______ *on the weather.*

e *She* ________ *up her flat every evening after work.*

f *That mobile phone* _______ *to Magda.*

g *He never* _________ *off his hat in class.*

3 Write to, for, up, on or off.

What time do you usually get up*?*

a *Come* ________*! Please walk faster.*

b *Can you ask your boss* ________ *more money?*

c *Her husband depends* _________ *her.*

d *My boss wants to speak* _______ *me.*

e *At work, do you have to put* ______ *a suit for meetings?*

f *Don't forget to thank them* ______ *inviting you to lunch.*

g *He never cleans* _______ *his bedroom.*

4 Work with a classmate. Write seven questions you can ask your partner using the verbs + prepositions in this unit. Ask and answer the questions.

For example:

A: *Do you wash up after meals?*

B: *No, I don't. My husband washes up.*

24

Uses of *like*

Database 1, 18

Cheng
Do you like English food?

Read these conversations. Look at the green words.

A: "Do you like English food?"
B: "Yes, I do. Some of it is very nice."

A: "Would you like a cup of tea?"
B: "Yes, please. Milk but no sugar for me."

A: "What's the weather like in your country?
B: "It's hot and sunny in the summer and it rains a lot in the winter."

Use in context

How do we use *like*? (page 100)

A Complete the examples.

1 ***We can use like to talk about things we enjoy or feel good about using Do you like?***
"Do you like English food?" "Yes, I ______."

2 ***We can use like to make an offer using Would you like?***
"______________________ a cup of tea?" "Yes, please."

3 ***We can use like to describe people, places or things using (What) is it like?***
"______________________ in your country?" "It's hot and sunny."

Practice

1 What type of questions are these? Write 1, 2 or 3 in each box.

1 ***Enjoy (Do you like?)*** **2** ***Offer (Would you like?)*** **3** ***Description (Is it like?)***

Do you like apples? [1]

a *What's your country like?* [ ]

b *Would you like a biscuit?* [ ]

c *Would you like to see a film tonight?* [ ]

d *Do you like watching football?* [ ]

e *What's the weather like today?* [ ]

f *What music does your sister like?* [ ]

g *What's your sister like?* [ ]

h *Why don't you like your class?* [ ]

i *Where would you like to go?* [ ]

j *What music would you like to listen to?* [ ]

k *What's your house like?* [ ]

2 Match the questions on the left with their answers on the right.

a *Do you like coffee?*	**1** *Go shopping, I think.*
b *Would you like anything more to eat?*	**2** *It's got two bedrooms and a nice view.*
c *Do you like watching TV?*	**3** *No, I don't. I prefer tea.*
d *Is your country like England?*	**4** *Anything I can dance to.*
e *What would you like to do this afternoon?*	**5** *No, thank you.*
f *What kind of music do you like?*	**6** *No, it isn't. It's very different.*
g *What's your new flat like?*	**7** *Not really. I'm more like my mother.*
h *Are you like your father?*	**8** *Yes, if there's a good programme on.*

3 Circle the correct word, do or would.

A: Do / Would you like a drink?
B: Yes, please. I'm really thirsty.

a *A: Do / Would you like your job?* — *B: Yes, it's very interesting.*

b *A: Do / Would you like getting up early?* — *B: It's OK. It isn't a problem for me.*

c *A: Do / Would you like to go out this evening?* — *B: No, I'd prefer to stay in.*

d *A: Do / Would you like the summer or the winter?* — *B: I love the summer.*

e *A: Where do / would you like to go on holiday?* — *B: I'd like to go to Italy.*

4 What is it / are they like? Write one word on each line to complete these questions and answers.

A: What's London like?
B: It's very big and busy.

a *A: What ____ Birmingham ________?* — *B: ____ ____ very nice.*

b *A: _____ _____ your parents _____?* — *B: _____ _____ very kind.*

c *A: _____ _____ your last holiday _____?* — *B: _____ _____ great, thanks!*

d *A: _____ _____ the weather _____ yesterday?* — *B: _____ _____ cold and grey.*

e *A: _____ _____ your brother _____?* — *B: _____ _____ tall and friendly.*

5 Work with a classmate. Ask and answer questions. Find out what your partner enjoys (do you like?), make offers (would you like?) and ask for descriptions (is it like?).

For example:

What do you like to eat?

Would you like to meet for a cup of coffee?

What's your country like?

25 was / were

past simple 1

Use in context

Jeya and Deva

They were in London.

Read these four conversations. Look at the green words.

A: "Where were you last night?"
B: "I was in bed because I wasn't very well."

A: "Where was Magda yesterday?"
B: "She was at the university."

A: "Where were Deva and Jeya on Saturday?"
B: "They weren't at home. They were in London."

How do we use was, were? (page 100)

Complete the tables.

1 *Was* **and** *were* **are the past of** *be.*

I	was	wasn't (was not)
you	*were*	________
he / she / it	________	*wasn't*
we	________	*weren't (were not)*
they	*were*	________

2 ***Questions***

Was	I ?
________	*you?*
________	*he / she / it?*
________	*we?*
________	*they?*

Practice

1 Circle the correct option.

I was / were very tired last night.

a *You was / were late for work today.*

b *The film wasn't / weren't very good.*

c *Was / Were there lots of people at the party?*

d *Marilyn Monroe was / were a famous film star.*

e *We was / were in Manchester last weekend.*

f *There wasn't / weren't anything in the fridge.*

g *Who was / were your last teacher?*

2 Correct these sentences.

I ~~were~~ at college yesterday evening. was

a *My mother were pleased to see me.*

b *The weather weren't sunny on holiday.*

c *The shopping bill didn't was correct.*

d *Was you tired after your journey?*

e *Did she was happy in her country?*

f *Did they was busy yesterday?*

g *Were Jan in class on Wednesday?*

3 Complete these conversations with the correct form of was or were.

a *A:* Were *you ill yesterday?* *B: Yes I ______. I ______ in bed.*

b *A: ______ the weather good in London?* *B: No, it ______. It ______ grey and wet.*

c *A: ______ those shoes expensive?* *B: No, they ______. They ______ in a sale.*

d *A: ______ Rafiq late for work?* *B: Yes, he ______. There ______ a traffic accident.*

e *A: ______ the post office open?* *B: No, it ______. It ______ closed.*

f *A: ______ your keys in your pocket?* *B: No, they ______. They ______ in my bag.*

g *A: ______ the restaurant OK?* *B: Yes, it ______. The food ______ delicious.*

h *A: ______ your exam hard?* *B: No, it ______. It ______ easy.*

4 Work with a classmate. Think of five questions using was and were to ask and answer.

For example:

Where were you at six o'clock last night?

Was the weather good on Sunday?

Were your trainers expensive?

When was the last time you were ill?

Were you at home on Saturday?

26 Regular verbs

past simple 2

Database 16

Use in context

Petra

Petra is waiting for Jan at the cinema. Look at the green words.

Jan: I'm sorry I'm late.
Petra: Did you walk here?
Jan: Yes, I did. I waited for the bus for 20 minutes but it didn't arrive.
Petra: OK, don't worry. The film only started a few minutes ago. We can still go in.

The film only started a few minutes ago.

How do we use regular verbs in the simple past? (page 100)

A **Complete the examples.**

1 ***In positive sentences, past regular verbs end in ~ed.***
wait → waited, start → ___________

2 ***In negative sentences, we use didn't + verb (not ~ed).***
I waited for the bus for 20 minutes but it __________ ________.

3 ***In questions, we use did + subject + verb (not ~ed).***
_____ you ______ here?

4 ***In short answers, we use did / didn't.***
Yes, I ______. No, I didn't.

Practice

1 **There are three different ways of pronouncing past ~ed endings. Complete the past forms of these verbs. Then say them aloud.**

(/ɪd/) waited /weɪtɪd/		
wait → waited	visit → ______	start → ______
need → ______	hate → ______	decide → ______
study → studied	copy → ______	

(/d/) loved /lʌvd/		
love → loved	live → ______	phone → ______
arrive → ______	die → ______	move → ______
close → ______	call → ______	clean → ______
try → tried	reply → ______	play → played
stay → ______		

(/t/) watched /wɒtʃt/		
watch → watched	wash → ______	crash → ______
finish → ______	walk → ______	talk → ______
work → ______	pick → ______	cook → ______
help → ______	like → ______	stop → stopped
drop → ______		

2 **Some of these sentences are correct and some are wrong. Tick (✓) the ones that are right and correct the mistakes in the other sentences.**

He ~~studyed~~ medicine at university. studied

a *She phoned me at nine o'clock last night.* ______

b *Did you watch television last night?* ______

c *She didn't enjoyed the film.* ______

d *She picked up the children after school.* ______

e *He lived not in the United States three years ago.* ______

f *What time you did finish work yesterday?* ______

g *I visited India in the winter.* ______

3 Look at these questions. Complete the answers.

A: *Did she like her present?* B: *Yes, she* did. *She* liked *it very much.*

a A: *Did you study English at school?* B: *Yes, I __________. I __________ it for two years.*

b A: *Did the train arrive on time?* B: *Yes, it __________. It __________ a little early.*

c A: *Did it stop raining on Saturday?* B: *No, it __________. It __________ all day.*

d A: *Did he help you with your English?* B: *Yes, he __________. He __________ me a lot.*

e A: *Did you talk to your family on the phone?* B: *Yes, I __________. I __________ to them for 15 minutes.*

4 Look at these questions and answers. Complete the questions.

A: *When* did *you* start *at college?* B: *I started at college three weeks ago.*

a A: *__________ you __________ her last night?* B: *No, I didn't phone her.*

b A: *Where __________ you __________ at the weekend?* B: *I stayed with my cousin.*

c A: *What __________ you __________ last night?* B: *I cooked chicken and rice.*

d A: *Why __________ you __________ to come to England?* B: *I decided to come here to get a job.*

e A: *__________ you __________ here?* B: *Yes, I did. I walked here.*

5 Work with a classmate. Ask and answer questions in the simple past.

Use work, live, study, stay, play, watch, enjoy, arrive, phone, walk and talk.

For example:

A: *Did you play football at school?*

B: *No, I didn't. I played basketball.*

27 Irregular verbs

past simple 3

Database 16

Magda

Jan is asking Magda about her holiday. Look at the green words.

Jan: Did you have a good holiday?

Magda: Yes, thanks, I did. I had a great time. I went home to Poland. I saw my family and I met all my old friends. I flew back yesterday and I didn't get back until one this morning.

I had a great time. I went home to Poland.

How do we use irregular verbs in the simple past? (page 101)

Complete the examples.

1. ***In positive sentences, past regular verbs have different endings.***
   have → had, go → ________, see → ________, meet → ______, fly → ________
2. ***In negative sentences, we use didn't + verb.*** *I ______ ______ back until one this morning.*
3. ***In questions, we use did + subject + verb.*** *______ you ______ a good holiday?*
4. ***In short answers, we use did / didn't.*** *Yes thanks, I ______. No, I didn't.*

Practice

1 **Look at the word chain, find the verbs and write the correct past form of each verb.**

gotmadediddrovetookspokeboughtknewputunderstoodthoughtleftatecamegavereadsoldsatslepttold

know knew

a *do* _______ **b** *come* _______ **c** *get* _______ **d** *give* _______

e *take* _______ **f** *leave* _______ **g** *sell* _______ **h** *drive* _______

i *understand* _______ **j** *make* _______ **k** *eat* _______ **l** *sleep* _______

m *put* _______ **n** *think* _______ **o** *read* _______ **p** *tell* _______

q *speak* _______ **r** *buy* _______ **s** *sit* _______

2 **Complete these conversations with one word in each line.**

A: What did you have for lunch? *B: I* had *a sandwich.*

a *A: Did you speak to your family on the phone?* *B: Yes, I _______ to my parents.*

b *A: Did you _______ about the exam?* *B: Yes, I knew about it.*

c *A: What time _____ you get home?* *B: I _____ home at 8.30.*

d *A: What _____ you _____ on Saturday?* *B: I bought some new shoes.*

e *A: _____ you understand the lesson?* *B: No, I _____________ _____________ it.*

f *A: _____ you drive to London or _____ you go by train?* *B: I _______ _______ there, I _______ by train.*

3 **Complete these conversations using the past forms of the verbs in the box. You can use each verb more than once.**

have	*go*	*do*	*see*	*make*	*swim*	*sleep*	*get*

a *A:* Did *you* have *a good holiday?* *B: Yes thanks, I _________ a great time.*

A: Where _______ you _________? *B: I _________ to my home country.*

A: What _________ you _________? *B: I _________ my family and I _________ some new friends.*

I _________ to the beach and I _________ every day.

b *A: What _____ you _____ at the weekend?* *B: I _________ _________ anything special.*

I _______ to the cinema on Saturday and I _______ a good film.

A: _______ you _____ out on Sunday? *B: No, I _______ all morning. I _______ up late, _______ a bath and then I _______ my homework. I _______ to bed early.*

4 **Work with a classmate. Ask and answer questions, for example, about your last holiday, what you did yesterday, last weekend.**

8 Present continuous / will (won't) / going to future

Database 1

Use in context

Jomo
We're going to have a party.

Pawel and Jomo are talking about their plans for the weekend. Look at the green words.

Pawel: What are you doing at the weekend, Jomo?
Jomo: I'm meeting some friends in London. We're going to have a party.
Pawel: When are you coming back?
Jomo: I'll probably come back on Sunday afternoon. What about you?
Pawel: I'm going to stay in and study. I'm taking my exams on Monday. But I'll probably go out on Saturday night.
Jomo: OK, I won't see you at the weekend but good luck with the exams. I'll see you next week!

How do we use will (won't), going to and present continuous? (page 101)

A **Complete the examples.**

1 ***We use will (won't) for future actions.***
A: I'll probably come back on Sunday afternoon.
B: I_____ probably ____ out on Saturday night.
A: OK, I_____ see you at the weekend. I___ ______ you next week!

2 ***We use going to for future intentions.***
A: We_____ ________ ______ ______ a party.
B: I__ _________ ___ ______ in and study.

3 ***We use present continuous for future arrangements.***
A: What ____ you ________ at the weekend?
B: I___ ________ some friends in London.
A: When _____ you ________ back?
B: I___ _________ my exams on Monday.

Practice

1 **Match a sentence on the left with a response on the right.**

a *Bye!*
b *What are you doing on Saturday?*
c *What time are we meeting?*
d *I don't feel very well.*
e *It's very hot in here.*
f *When will the exam finish?*
g *Can I see the doctor this morning?*

1 *I'm not sure. I'll phone you later and tell you.*
2 *It'll finish at 12.30.*
3 *I'll open a window.*
4 *Bye! I'll see you later.*
5 *Sit down. I'll get you some water.*
6 *I'll probably go shopping.*
7 *I'll give you an appointment for 9 o'clock.*

2 **Complete these sentences with** *~'s / ~'re going to.*

It's going to *rain.*

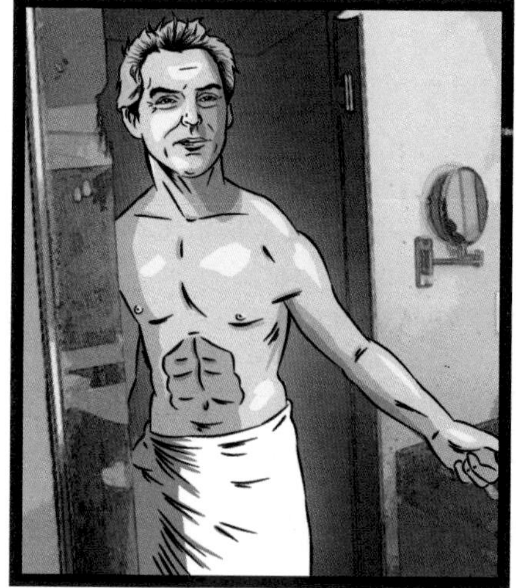

a *He* __________________ *have a shower.*

b *They* __________________ *play tennis.*

c *He* __________________ *be a racing driver.*

d *She ____________________ take a taxi.* **e** *They ____________________ paint the kitchen.*

3 Deva is going into hospital for an operation. Complete the questions and answers about the arrangements using the present continuous.

Jeya: *When are you having your operation?* **Deva:** *I'm having it on Wednesday.*

Jeya: *When are you going into hospital?* **Deva:** *I___ ________ in on Wednesday morning.*

Jeya: *Who is taking you to hospital?* **Deva:** *Rafiq___ _________ me.*

Jeya: *How long are you staying?* **Deva:** *I___ ___________ overnight.*

Jeya: *Who is picking up the children from school?* **Deva:** *My sister____ _________up the children.*

Jeya: *Who is looking after the children?* **Deva:** *Rafiq____ __________ after them.*

Jeya: *When ______ you __________ home?* **Deva:** *I'm coming home on Thursday afternoon.*

Jeya: *When ______ you _________ back to work?* **Deva:** *I'm not going back to work for two weeks.*

4 Work with a classmate. Ask and answer questions about future actions, intentions and plans.

must / mustn't / have to

obligation

Ismail is talking about his job. Look at the green words.

"I start work at 8.00. I mustn't be late so I have to get up at 6.30. In my last job I didn't have to get up until 7.30 but I had to wear a suit and tie. I don't have to wear a suit now, but I must look smart and tidy. Sorry, I must go now – I'll be late!"

How do we use must / mustn't / have to?

(page 101)

Complete the examples.

1 ***When something is necessary, we use have to or must.***
I have to get up at 6.30. I ________ look smart and tidy. I ________ go now.

2 ***When something is not necessary, we use don't (doesn't) have to.***
I ________________ wear a suit now.

3 ***When something is the wrong thing to do, we use mustn't.***
I __________ be late.

4 ***The past of must and have to is had to (didn't have to).***
I ____________________ get up till 7.30 but I ________________ wear a suit and tie.

Practice

1 Correct the mistakes in these sentences.

I must ~~to~~ post these letters. I must post these letters.

a *I must to check my e-mails.* ______

b *You don't must phone the office before 9 a.m.* ______

c *I have wear special clothes in my job.* ______

d *When I was at school, I must wear a uniform.* ______

e *He don't have to travel in his job.* ______

f *You mustn't to smoke in restaurants in England.* ______

g *I didn't must pay for the coffee because my friend paid for me.* ______

2 Match the questions on the left with their answers on the right.

a *Are we late?*
b *Do I have to do a test?*
c *Is he still sleeping?*
d *How many tablets must I take?*
e *Do you have to work at the weekends?*
f *Did the doctor see you?*
g *Is there a message for me?*
h *Did you have to pay for your course?*

1 *Yes, you mustn't wake him up.*
2 *Yes, but we had to wait half an hour.*
3 *Yes, you must hurry up.*
4 *No, I didn't have to – it was free.*
5 *Yes, you have to phone your mother.*
6 *I sometimes have to work on Saturdays.*
7 *Everyone has to do an exam this term.*
8 *You have to take three a day.*

3 Choose the best answer, mustn't or don't have to.

You mustn't / don't have to smoke in pubs in England.

a *You mustn't / don't have to drive on the right in England.*

b *Most people mustn't / don't have to get up early on Sundays.*

c *You mustn't / don't have to use a car if you can walk to work.*

d *You mustn't / don't have to eat chip sandwiches if you want to lose weight.*

e *In England, people under 17 years old mustn't / don't have to drive cars.*

f *Young people in England mustn't / don't have to do military service.*

4 Write one word on each line to complete these questions and answers.

a A: *Are you ready for your interview?* B: *Yes, I* must *go, I ________ be late.*

b A: *How often ____ you ______ to see the dentist?* B: *I ______ to go every three months.*

c A: *Is there anything you _____ ___ do tonight?* B: *Yes, I _______ do the ironing.*

d A: *______ you ______ ____ get any shopping?* B: *Yes, I _____ get some eggs and milk.*

e A: *Did you _____ ___ wear a uniform when you were at school?* B: *No, I _____ _____ to.*

f A: *_____ you _______ ____ get up early yesterday?* B: *Yes, I _____ ____ get up at 5 o'clock.*

5 Work with a classmate. Ask and answer questions using must, have to and had to. Ask about things you have to do, places you have to go and things you had to do in the past, for example, when you were at school.

For example:

A: *Do you have to do anything tomorrow?*

B: *Yes, I have to go to work.*

A: *Did you have to play sports at school?*

B: *Yes, we had to play volleyball.*

6 Now write a short paragraph about your daily life using must, mustn't and have to.

For example:
I have to get up at 7 o'clock. I mustn't be late for school.

____

____

____

____

____

____

____

Comparative adjectives

Database 2

Use in context

Rafiq

Rafiq is talking about life in England. Look at the green words.

"In some ways, life in England is better than in my country, Sri Lanka. There are more opportunities here for me. I have a better job and I work harder here, so my family can live in a bigger house and we can have a more comfortable life. But life here is busier and more expensive. Also the weather is warmer in Sri Lanka and I think the country is more beautiful. So, in some ways, life for me is worse in this country than at home."

The weather is warmer in Sri Lanka.

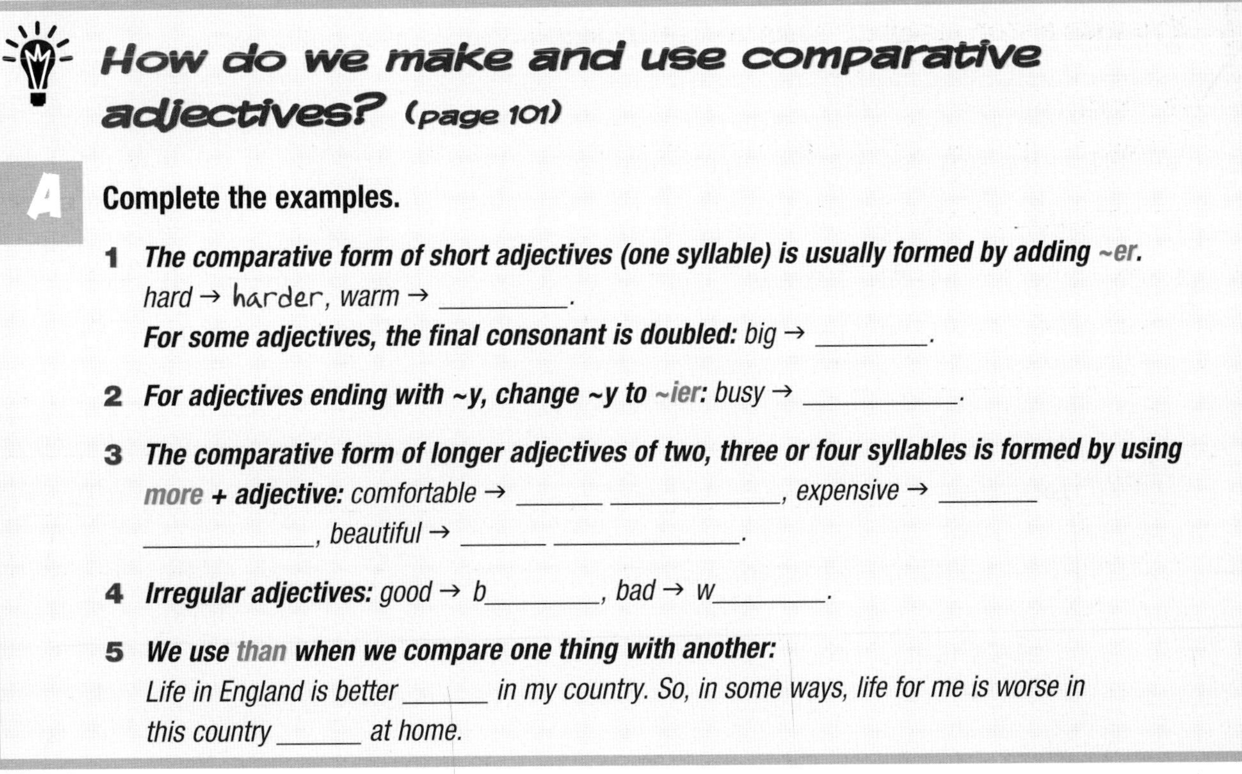

How do we make and use comparative adjectives? (page 101)

A Complete the examples.

1 ***The comparative form of short adjectives (one syllable) is usually formed by adding ~er.***
hard → harder, *warm* → __________.
For some adjectives, the final consonant is doubled: *big* → ________.

2 ***For adjectives ending with ~y, change ~y to ~ier:*** *busy* → ____________.

3 ***The comparative form of longer adjectives of two, three or four syllables is formed by using more + adjective:*** *comfortable* → ______ ____________, *expensive* → ________ ____________, *beautiful* → ______ ____________.

4 ***Irregular adjectives:*** *good* → *b*________, *bad* → *w*________.

5 ***We use than when we compare one thing with another:***
Life in England is better ______ *in my country. So, in some ways, life for me is worse in this country* ______ *at home.*

1 Write the comparatives of the words in the box in the correct column.

~~happy~~ important hot dark old serious fat near angry young comfortable dangerous sad heavy careful slim short interesting friendly easy fit

Short adjectives + ~er	Short adjectives, double consonant	Adjectives ending with ~y	Long adjectives
______	______	happier	______
______	______	______	______
______	______	______	______
______	______	______	______
______	______	______	______
______	______	______	______
______	______	______	______
______	______	______	______

2 Correct the adjectives in these sentences.

My country is ~~boter~~ than England. hotter

a *My new car is more fast than my last one.* ______

b *My wife is carefuller than me.* ______

c *Your bag is heavier that mine.* ______

d *I think my English is more good than three months ago.* ______

e *This restaurant is more nicer than the other one.* ______

f *The weather is badder than yesterday.* ______

g *This new chair is more comfortable then my old one.* ______

3 Look at the information about two students. Write sentences to compare Jan with Roman.

Jan is 27. Roman is 22. Jan is older than Roman.

a *Jan is 1 metre 64 centimetres tall. Roman is 1 metre 69 centimetres tall. Roman is* __________ __________ *Jan.*

b *Jan is serious. Roman isn't serious. Jan is* _______ _____________ _______ *Roman.*

c *Jan speaks good English. Roman doesn't speak English well. Jan speaks* _________ *English* _______ *Roman.*

d *Jan works hard. Roman doesn't work hard. Jan* _________ ________________ _________ *Roman.*

e *Jan is careful. Roman isn't careful. Jan* _______ ________ _______________ _______ *Roman.*

f *Jan isn't very happy. Roman is always happy. Roman* ________ ________________ _________ *Jan.*

4 Work with a classmate. Ask and answer questions. Ask how your partner's life compares with life in his or her country. Ask about how they compare with someone else in their family.

For example:

A: *Do you think life is better in this country?*

B: *In some ways it's better, for example we are richer.*

A: *Is your sister older than you?*

B: *Yes, she's three years older than me.*

1 am / is / are: the verb be 1

We can use the verb be to talk about personal information, for example:

- *name: My name is Deva. I'm Deva.*
- *country: I'm from Sri Lanka.*
- *nationality: I'm Sri Lankan.*
- *age: I'm 32 years old. My son is eight.*
- *marital status: I'm married. I'm single. I'm divorced.*
- *job: He's a taxi driver.*
- *family: We are a small family of four people.*
- *feelings: Sometimes life isn't easy but we're happy.*

2 there is / there are / it is / they are: the verb be 2

We use:

there is or there are to talk about things or people generally.
there is for one thing or person: There's a supermarket.
there are for more than one thing or person: There are lots of families with young children in our street.
it is when we know the special thing or person: It's (the supermarket's) a big shop with everything I need.
they are when we know the special things or people: They (the families) are all very friendly.

3 The present continuous

We use the present continuous to talk about:

- *something that is happening right now: Rafiq is working.*
- *the general present situation: Amir's looking for a job.*
- *future arrangements: I'm working tomorrow morning.*

To form the present continuous we add ~ing to the verb:
jump – jump + ing = jumping, walk – walk + ing = walking, stay + ing = staying
For verbs ending in ~e, remove the 'e' and add ~ing:
live – live + ing = living, come – come + ing = coming
For some verbs we need to double the final consonant before adding ~ing:
shop – shop + p + ing = shopping, run – run + n + ing = running
For verbs ending in ~ie, remove the 'ie' and add 'y' before adding ~ing:
die – d + y + ing = dying, lie – l + y + ing = lying

4 I / you / we / they: present simple 1

We use the present simple to talk about:

- *activities every day, most days, often, sometimes, generally:* I go to work.
- *true information:* She lives in London.

We use some verbs in the simple form, not the continuous, all the time.
For example: know – I know ~~(I'm knowing)~~*. We call these state or stative verbs. The following are all stative verbs:* agree, believe, forget, remember, think *(= believe),* understand, like, hate, need, prefer, want, hear, see, smell, taste, belong, cost.

5 he / she / it: present simple 2

The pronunciation of ~s and ~es endings:

- *Words ending in ~se: close → clos**es** /kləʊzɪz/ use → us**es** /juːzɪz/*
- *Words ending in ~sh: finish → finish**es** /fɪnɪʃɪz/ brush → brush**es** /brʌʃɪz/ wash → wash**es** /wɒʃɪz/*
- *Words ending in ~ch: watch → watch**es** /wɒtʃɪz/ match → match**es** /mætʃɪz/ teach → teach**es** /tiːtʃɪz/*
- *Words ending in ~ss: pass → pass**es** /pɑːsɪz/ kiss → kiss**es** /kɪsɪz/*
- ***Words ending in ~ry, ~dy:** hurry → hurr**ies** /hʌrɪz/ carry → carr**ies** /kærɪz/ study → stud**ies** /stʌdɪz/*
- *Some other present simple verbs are formed by adding ~s to a verb ending in ~e, but the ~es is not pronounced as a separate syllable: live → liv**es** /lɪvz/ come → com**es** /kʌmz/ leave → leav**es** /liːvz/*

6 Imperatives

The imperative is formed by using the infinitive without 'to', for example: ~~to go~~ → go.
We use imperatives for:

- *instructions: Take two tablets three times a day.*
- *orders: Send them an e-mail.*
- *directions: Turn left at the traffic lights.*
- *invitations and offers: Please come in. Have another biscuit.*

7 Question words

Note the word order for making questions:

- *present continuous: Am I going? / Are you / we / they going? / Is he / she / it going?*
- *present simple: Do I / you / we / they go? Does he / she / it go?*

8 can / can't (cannot) / could / couldn't: modal verbs

We usually say can't but the full form is cannot (one word).
We use can for present ability: I can play the piano (now). For past ability we use could: I could play the piano when I was five.
We use can or could for present or future possibility: I can meet you at 6.00. / I could meet you at 6.00. There is little difference in meaning. Here, could is not the past of can.
We use can or could to ask someone for something: Can you help me, please? Could you post a letter for me? Again, there is little difference in meaning. Here, could is not the past of can.

9 have got

We never use have got for activities: I'm having a good time. (~~I have got a good time.~~)
British English uses have got more than American English, for example:

- ***British English:** A: Have you got a pen? B: Yes, I have.*
- ***American English:** A: Do you have a pen? B: Yes, I do.*

10 some / any: quantity 1

We usually use some in positive sentences and any in negative (not) sentences.
In questions, there is not a clear rule – sometimes we use some and sometimes any. If we use some, the question feels more positive and we expect the answer 'Yes': Have you got some money? (Yes, of course!) but we can also ask: Have you got any money? We often use some when we are offering something: Would you like some cake? We can also say: Would you like any cake?

11 how much / how many / a lot / a few / a little: quantity 2

We can count countable nouns, for example: one egg, two eggs, three eggs.
We can't count uncountable nouns, for example: milk, ~~two milks~~
With uncountable nouns, we often use another way of counting them, for example: two bottles of milk.
We use some nouns as countable and uncountable, for example: I'd like two coffees, please. (two cups of coffee = countable). I need to buy some coffee. (a kilo of coffee = uncountable).

12 Making plurals: nouns

The plurals of these commonly used nouns are exceptions to the normal rules:
potato → potatoes, tomato → tomatoes, man → men, woman → women, child → children, person → people, tooth → teeth, foot → feet, mouse → mice, sheep → sheep, fish → fish.

13 a / an / the: articles

We use a/an when we talk generally: Would you like an apple? (There are many apples on the plate, please take one.) We use the when there is one special thing or person we are talking about: Would you like the apple? (There is one apple on the plate.) We can also use the with plural nouns: The trains in France are really fast.
In English we usually use a/an and not one: I've got a house. (~~I've got one house.~~) We usually use one in answer to How many? – I've got one car (not two).

14 the: the definite article

We use the before these countries, states and unions:

- The United…, for example: The United Kingdom, The United States, The United Arab Emirates.
- The Republic of…, for example: The Republic of Ireland, The People's Republic of China, The Netherlands, The Seychelles.
- The … Union, for example: The European Union.

We use the to talk generally about some activities, for example: I like the cinema/the theatre. We use the to talk about some places, for example: I'm going to the bank/the post office/the doctor's/the dentist's/the station/the airport/the city centre.
We don't use the to talk about these general activities:

- I go to bed/work/school/college/church. She is in prison/hospital. He is at home.

15 this / that / these / those: demonstratives

Some other common uses of this and that:

- On the phone: A: Who's that? / Is that Omi? B: Yes, this is Omi speaking.
- Introducing someone: 'This is my brother, Saeed.'
- A: Thank you. B: That's OK. / That's all right. / That's fine.
- A: I'm getting married. B: That's great! / That's nice.

16 Pronouns

Subject	Object	Possessive	
I have a car	It belongs to me	It's my car	It's mine
I	me	my	mine
you	you	your	yours
he	him	his	his
she	her	her	hers
we	us	our	ours
they	them	their	theirs

18 Adverbs

Regular adverbs are formed using adjective + ly: clear → clearly.

- Adjectives ending with ~y change to ~ily: easy → easily, angry → angrily, heavy → heavily, hungry → hungrily
- Adjectives ending with ~ful change to ~fully: careful → carefully, beautiful → beautifully

Irregular adverbs: good → well

- *These adverbs are the same as the adjectives: fast → fast, late → late, early → early, hard → hard*
- *Notice that the adverb hardly means very little:*
  He works hard = He works a lot. He hardly works = He works very little.

19 Prepositions of time: in / on / at

in	on	at
months, seasons, years, the morning, the afternoon, the evening	*part of a day, days, dates*	*times, the weekend, night, at the moment festival holidays (Christmas)*

Note: We say in the morning, but on Tuesday morning, at night but on Friday night.

20 Prepositions of place: in / on / at

in	on	at
a room, a flat, a house, an office, a building a street, a town, a city the town/city centre a region a car, a taxi	*a floor the coast a bus, a train, a plane*	*an address (a number) a school, a college, a university, a workplace*

22 Prepositional phrases

to	on	by	at	in
go to / get to a place, go to bed	*on time on the phone, the computer on business go on holiday on foot get on/off the bus, train, plane on TV, the radio*	*go by bus, car, train, boat, plane*	*be at home, work, school, college be at the station, airport be at a party, a match*	*be in bed, in hospital, in prison, in the world*

23 Verbs + prepositions

Some verbs are normally followed by prepositions:

- *to: listen, belong, write, talk, speak*
- *for: wait, ask (someone) for (something), thank (someone) for (something)*
- *on: switch on/off, turn on/off, depend on, rely on*

Some verbs + prepositions have special meanings. These are phrasal verbs or expressions. For example:

- *up: pick (someone) up, hurry, get, clean, tidy, wash*
- *on: come, go, put on/take off*

Some phrasal verbs can be followed by different prepositions with different meanings, for example, look: look after = take care of, look at = watch, look for = try to find

24 Uses of like

We normally use the verb to like in the simple form: Do you like? / I like / I don't like (~~I am liking~~).
We can also use the verb to like with 'would' to make an offer – Would you like? – or to say what we want – I'd like (I'd like to go for a coffee.)
In the sentence 'What's (is) it like?' the word like is not a verb and it has a different meaning. It means 'similar to'. We use What's it like? to ask someone to tell us how something is, to describe it. So, 'What's the weather like?' is asking how the weather is, not if you enjoy it. The answer is, for example, 'It's hot and sunny', not, 'I like the weather'.
We can also use like to ask about people, for example:

- *A: What's your brother like? B: He's tall and friendly.*
- *A: Are you like (similar to) your brother? B: No, my brother and I are very different.*

25 was / were: past simple 1

We use simple past for finished actions or times.
The past of is / are:

- *I / he / she / it was / wasn't (was not)*
- *you / we / they were / weren't (were not)*

Questions about the past:

- *Was I / he / she / it? (~~Did he was~~)*
- *Were you / we / they? (~~Did you were~~)*

26 Regular verbs: past simple 2:

Positive	Negative	Questions
I started *You started* *He / She / It started* *We started* *They started*	*I didn't (did not) start* *You didn't start* *He / She / It didn't start* *We didn't start* *They didn't start*	*Did I start?* *Did you start?* *Did he / she / it start?* *Did we start?* *Did they start?*

27 Irregular verbs: past simple 3

See Database 16 for a list of irregular verbs.

Positive	Negative	Questions
I went	*I didn't (did not) go*	*Did I go?*
You went	*You didn't go*	*Did you go?*
He / She / It went	*He / She / It didn't go*	*Did he / she / it go?*
We went	*We didn't go*	*Did we go?*
They went	*They didn't go*	*Did they go?*

28 Present continuous / will / going to: future

will: *We use will for general future actions often if we are not 100% sure – I think I'll go to the party on Saturday – or with probably, definitely – I'll definitely phone you tonight. Sometimes we use will for a sudden decision – I've got five minutes free, so I'll phone George. The negative of will is won't (will not).*

going to: *We often use going to for things we want to do, have decided to do or intend to do. I'm going to travel round the world after I finish at college. We can say going to go but we often just say going to: I'm going to go to London at the weekend – I'm going to London at the weekend.*

We also use going to if we can see something is going to happen in the near future: The sky is very dark. It's going to rain.

present continuous: *We often use present continuous for appointments, dates and arrangements which are fixed. I'm playing football at 3.00 tomorrow afternoon.*

29 must / mustn't / have to: obligation

We use must and have to to say something is necessary. Generally, we use have to for laws, rules, something someone else tells us to do – You have to register with the police in this country – and we use must for more personal obligations – I must do some ironing – but the difference between using must and have to is very small.

We use don't/doesn't have to to say something is not necessary. We can also say needn't – I don't have to wear a suit = I needn't wear a suit.

Mustn't has a similar meaning to can't / not allowed to, or even, forbidden / prohibited.

You mustn't smoke in here = You can't smoke in here / You're not allowed to smoke in here / Smoking in here is forbidden / prohibited.

Must has only one form – the present. We can use it for the future, for example, I must phone my mother tomorrow, but we normally use have to for other tenses: I'll have to phone my mother tomorrow, I had to phone her yesterday.

30 Comparative adjectives

Adjectives ending consonant + vowel (a,e,i,o,u) + consonant: double the consonant to make the comparative: big → bigger, hot → hotter, sad → sadder, fat → fatter, fit → fitter

Two-syllable adjectives: some add –er, for example: quiet → quieter. But most comparatives are with more: more modern, more careful, more peaceful.

1 Activities and hobbies

In the house

We do: the housework, the cooking, the washing-up, the cleaning, the washing, the ironing, the shopping (we go shopping), the decorating.

At college, school or university

We study.
We do homework, self-study, a test, an exam, reading, writing, listening, speaking.

Sports

We do exercise, sport (sports).
We go jogging, running, swimming, cycling, riding, to the gym, fishing, racing.
We play football, tennis, volleyball, cricket, baseball, basketball.

Hobbies

We do gardening, DIY (the painting and decorating), painting.
We go to the cinema, the theatre.
We use the computer, we watch television, we listen to the radio.

Activities with do and go

We go shopping and we do sport. We do the shopping and we go running!

Put these activities in the correct column in the table.

the cooking	the housework	homework	swimming	the cleaning
exercise	jogging	fishing	the washing	travelling

do	go
sport, the shopping	shopping, running

2 Adjectives

Adjective	Comparative	Opposite adjective	Comparative
big	*bigger*	*small*	*smaller*
fast	*faster*	*slow*	*slower*
fat	*fatter*	*slim*	*slimmer*
fit	*fitter*	*unfit*	*more unfit*
good	*better**	*bad*	*worse**
hot	*hotter*	*cold*	*colder*
long	*longer*	*short*	*shorter*
near	*nearer*	*far*	*further/farther**
new	*newer*	*old*	*older*
nice	*nicer*	–	–
warm	*warmer*	*cool*	*cooler*
young	*younger*	*old*	*older*
angry	*angrier*	*calm*	*calmer*
busy	*busier*	*quiet*	*quieter*
easy	*easier*	*hard*	*harder*
friendly	*friendlier*	*unfriendly*	–
happy	*happier*	*sad*	*sadder*
heavy	*heavier*	*light*	*lighter*
beautiful	*more beautiful*	*ugly*	*uglier*
careful	*more careful*	*careless*	*more careless*
comfortable	*more comfortable*	*uncomfortable*	*more uncomfortable*
dangerous	*more dangerous*	*safe*	*safer*
important	*more important*	*unimportant*	–
interesting	*more interesting*	*boring*	*more boring*
modern	*more modern*	*old-fashioned*	*more old-fashioned*
serious	*more serious*	*happy*	*happier*

**irregular*

3 Britain

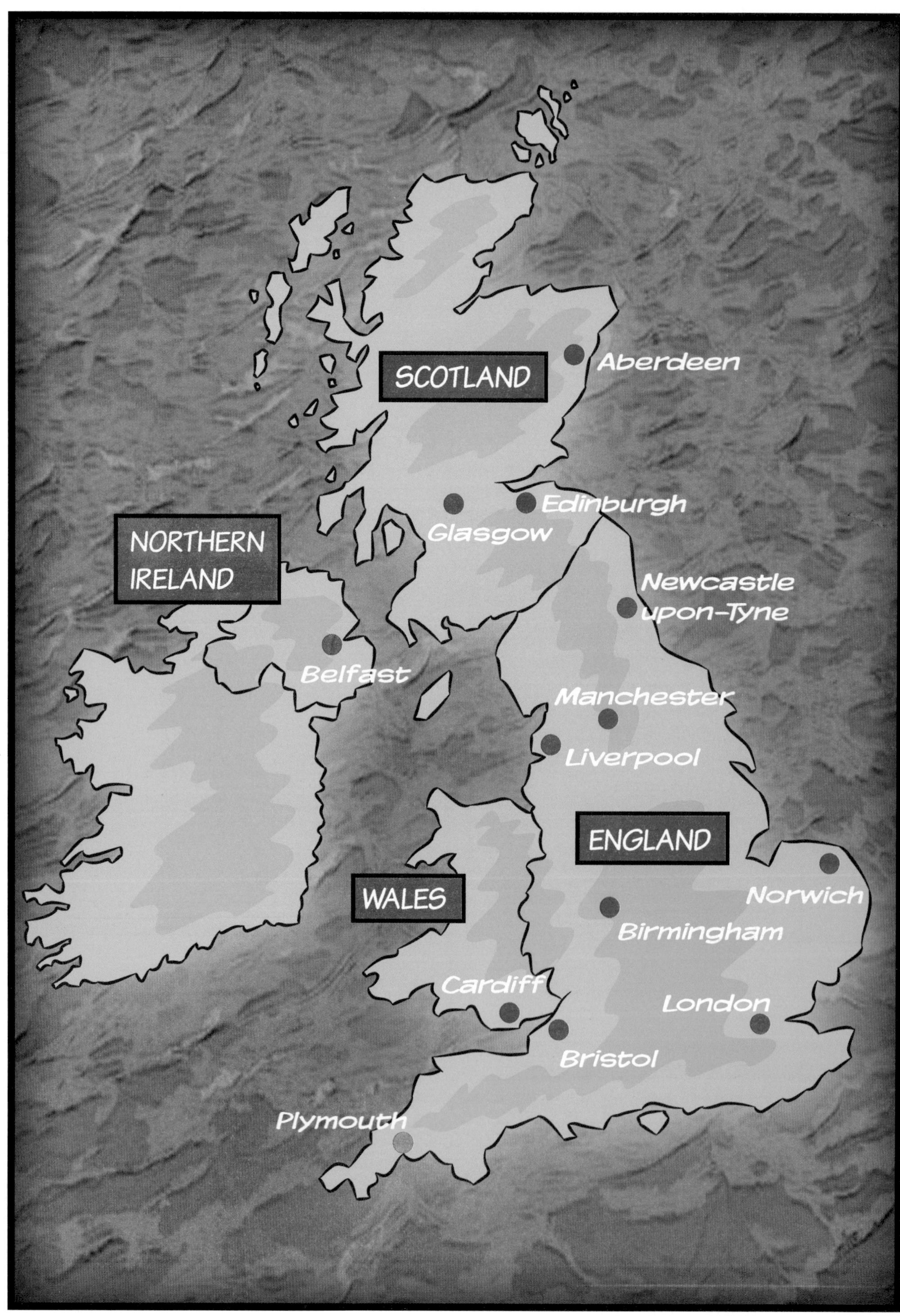

SCOTLAND
Aberdeen
Edinburgh
Glasgow
NORTHERN IRELAND
Newcastle upon-Tyne
Belfast
Manchester
Liverpool
ENGLAND
WALES
Norwich
Birmingham
Cardiff
London
Bristol
Plymouth

4 The café

Match the pictures and the words.

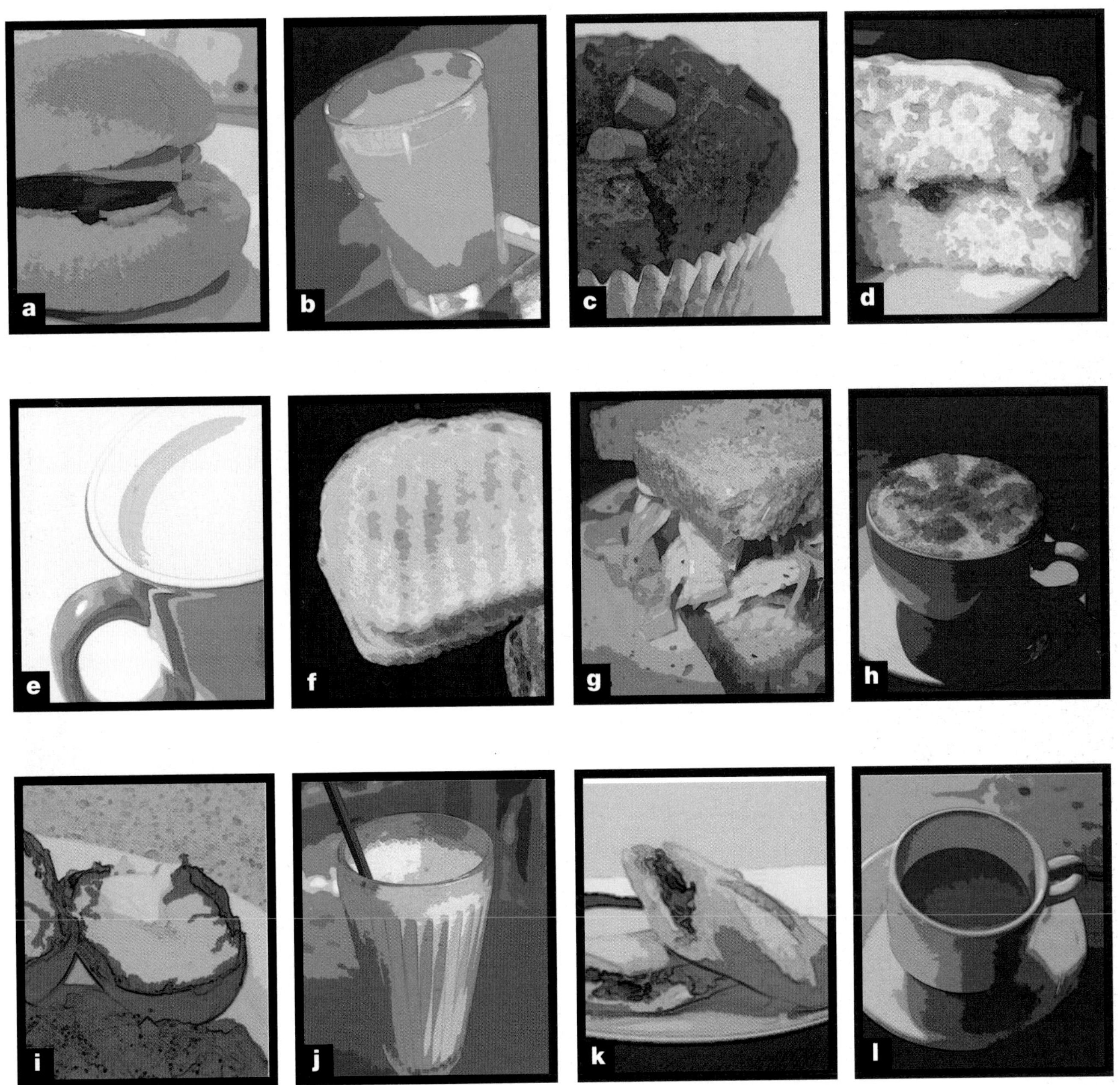

a mug of tea *a black coffee* *a milkshake* *a chicken salad sandwich* *a cheese roll* *a cappuccino*
a baguette with egg mayo *a muffin* *an orange juice* *a toasted sandwich* *a jacket potato* *a piece of cake*

5 Clothes

Match the pictures and the words.

shirt	*jacket*	*sweater*	*blouse*	*tights*	*socks*	*T-shirt*	*skirt*
slippers	*belt*	*shoes*	*jeans*	*tie*	*trousers*	*trainers*	

6 College subjects

Write the words in your own language.

science ______________ *physics* ______________ *chemistry* ______________

mathematics ______________ *geophysics* ______________ *biology* ______________

geography ______________ *geology* ______________ *biochemistry* ______________

business studies ______________ *computer science* ______________ *IT studies* ______________

programming ______________ *finance* ______________ *accountancy* ______________

bookkeeping ______________ *languages* ______________ *media studies* ______________

photography ______________

aeronautics ______________ *automotive engineering* ______________

mechanical engineering ______________ *electronics* ______________ *design* ______________

hairdressing ______________ *beauty therapy* ______________

7 Colours

white

yellow
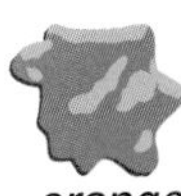
orange

red

purple

brown

blue

green

grey

black

8 Countries and nationalities

'I'm from Sri Lanka (country). I'm Sri Lankan (nationality).'

1 Match these European countries and nationalities.

Europe	European
a *United Kingdom*	**1** *Swiss*
b *France*	**2** *Portuguese*
c *Spain*	**3** *Czech*
d *Portugal*	**4** *Greek*
e *Italy*	**5** *French*
f *Switzerland*	**6** *Dutch*
g *Poland*	**7** *British*
h *The Netherlands*	**8** *Estonian*
i *The Czech Republic*	**9** *German*
j *Estonia*	**10** *Spanish*
k *Germany*	**11** *Polish*
l *Greece*	**12** *Italian*

2 What other European countries and nationalities can you think of?

__________ __________ __________ __________ __________

__________ __________ __________

3 What continent or country do these people come from?

Asian Asia

a *Egyptian* ________	**b** *Indian* ________	**c** *Pakistani* ________	**d** *Sudanese* ________
e *Somali* ________	**f** *Brazilian* ________	**g** *Taiwanese* ________	**h** *Russian* ________
i *Moroccan* ________	**j** *Thai* ________	**k** *Philippino* ________	**l** *Saudi Arabian* ________
m *Iraqi* ________	**n** *Japanese* ________	**o** *American* ________	**p** *Colombian* ________
q *Argentinian* ________	**r** *Indonesian* ________		

4 What are the countries and nationalities of the people in your class?

_______________ _______________ _______________ _______________ _______________

_______________ _______________ _______________

9 Days and months

1 Put the days in order. 1–7.

Wednesday ____ *Saturday* ____ *Monday* _1_ *Friday* ____ *Sunday* ____ *Tuesday* ____ *Thursday* ____

2 Put the months in order. 1–12.

September ____ *January* _1_ *December* ____ *March* ____ *July* ____ *February* ____ *October* ____

August ____ *April* ____ *June* ____ *November* ____ *May* ____

10 Directions to places

Write these words and sentences in your own language.

We use these verbs when we give directions:

Go: Go down this road.

_______________ ____

Turn: Turn left at the traffic lights.

_______________ ____

Take: Take the first road on the right.

_______________ ____

Continue / Carry on: Carry on up this street.

_______________ _______________ ____

We use these prepositions:

straight / straight ahead ______

down ______

up ______

along ______

over ______

under ______

across ______

by / near ______

next to ______

opposite ______

in front of ______

behind ______

We use these expressions (write these words in your own language):

as far as __________ *until/ till* __________ *left* __________ *right* __________ *on the left* __________

on the right __________ *You'll see it* __________ *You can't miss it!* __________

And these nouns:

road __________ *street* __________ *turning* __________ *traffic lights* __________ *junction* __________

roundabout __________

11 Food shopping

Write the words in your own language. Match the pictures to the food.

Meat

a

b

c

d

e

f

lamb ☐ __________	*beef* ☐ __________	*veal* ☐ __________
chicken ☐ __________	*turkey* ☐ __________	*pork* ☐ __________
ham ☐ __________	*bacon* ☐ __________	

Fruit

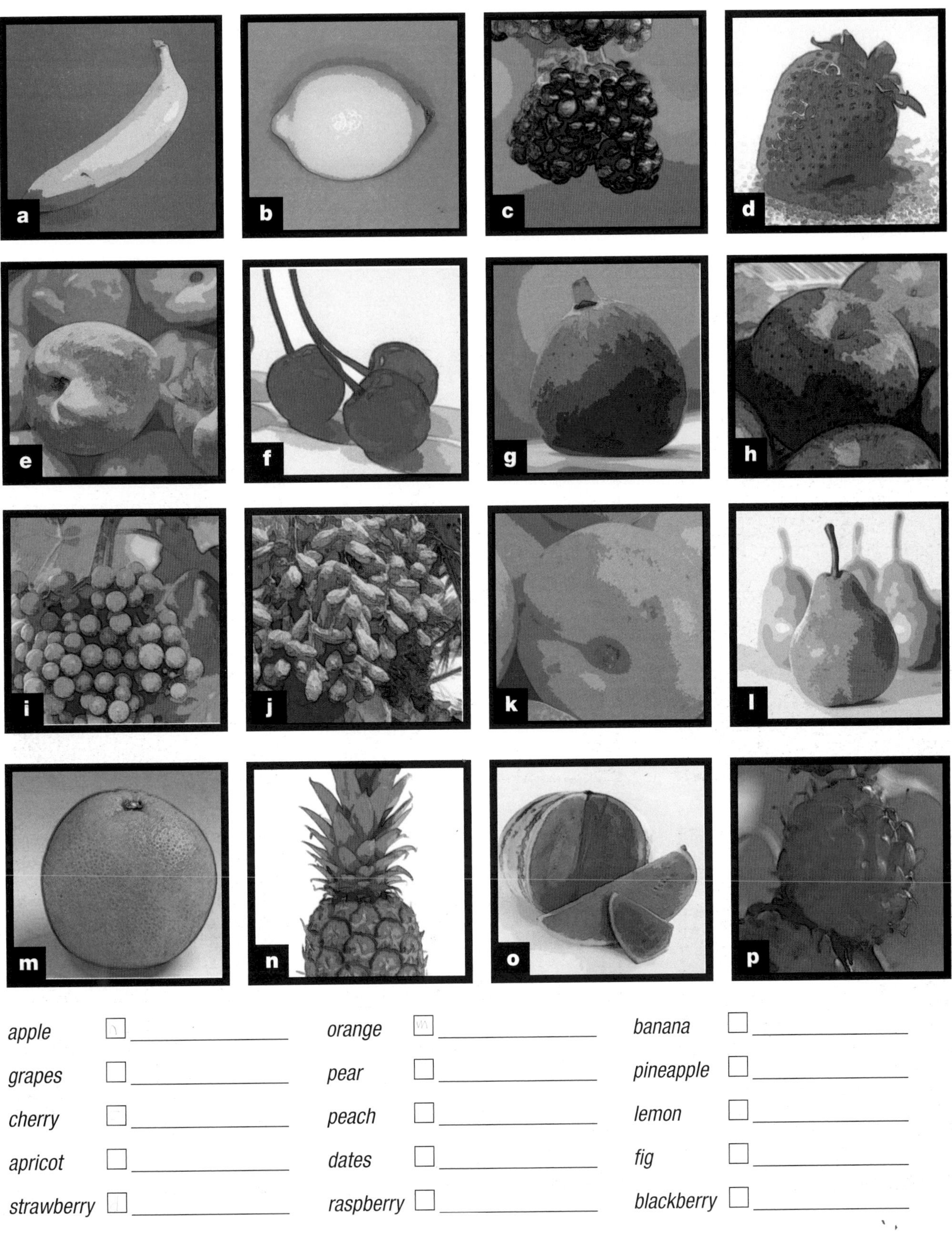

apple ☐ __________	*orange* ☐ __________	*banana* ☐ __________
grapes ☐ __________	*pear* ☐ __________	*pineapple* ☐ __________
cherry ☐ __________	*peach* ☐ __________	*lemon* ☐ __________
apricot ☐ __________	*dates* ☐ __________	*fig* ☐ __________
strawberry ☐ __________	*raspberry* ☐ __________	*blackberry* ☐ __________
melon ☐ __________		

Vegetables

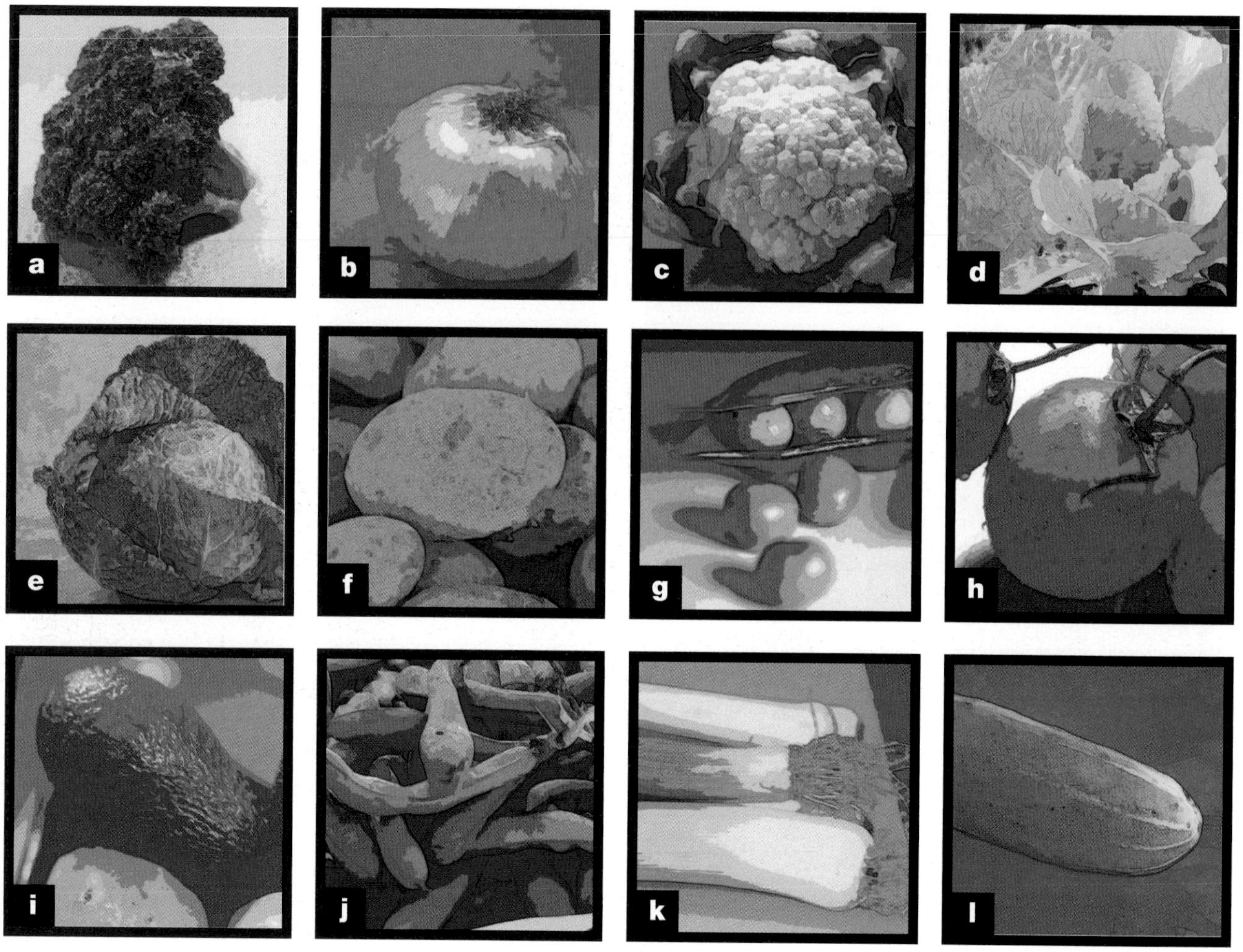

a b c d

e f g h

i j k l

potato ☐ ______	*beans* ☐ ______	*broccoli* ☐ ______
cauliflower ☐ ______	*peas* ☐ ______	*onion* ☐ ______
cabbage ☐ ______	*cucumber* ☐ ______	*tomato* ☐ ______
lettuce ☐ ______	*leek* ☐ ______	*avocado* ☐ ______

12 Furniture

1 Write the letters in the correct boxes.

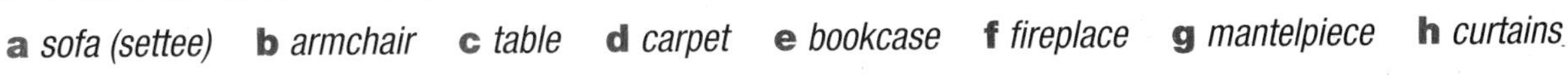

a *sofa (settee)* **b** *armchair* **c** *table* **d** *carpet* **e** *bookcase* **f** *fireplace* **g** *mantelpiece* **h** *curtains*

i *sink* **j** *worktop* **k** *cooker* **l** *oven* **m** *fridge* **n** *cupboard*
o *drawers* **p** *microwave* **q** *dishwasher* **r** *washing machine* **s** *tumble drier*

2 Write the letters in the correct boxes.

a *wardrobe* **b** *bed* **c** *bedside table* **d** *lamp* **e** *dressing table* **f** *mirror* **g** *chest of drawers*

h *basin* **i** *taps* **j** *shower* **k** *bath* **l** *toilet / W.C.* **m** *bidet* **n** *towel rail* **o** *stool*

13 Health

Write these words and sentences in your own language.

Medicines

Medicine can be:

tablets ______ ***pills*** ______ ***capsules*** ______

*Take two **tablets** three times a day.*

______

syrup, medicine *Take one 5ml spoonful of this **medicine** before meals.*

______ ______ ______

ointment, lotion, cream *Apply this **ointment** to the affected area as needed.*

______ ______ ______

Useful words and expressions

a dose ______ *dosage* ______

Do not exceed the stated dose. ______

Once opened, keep refrigerated. ______

Do not use if the seal is broken. ______

symptoms ______ *If symptoms persist, consult your doctor.* ______

once ______ *twice* ______ *a course of tablets* ______

antibiotics ______

The face

a ______
b ______
c ______
d ______
e ______
f ______
g ______
h ______
i ______
j ______
k ______
l ______

head hair ear eye eyebrow nose lips teeth chin cheek neck throat

The body

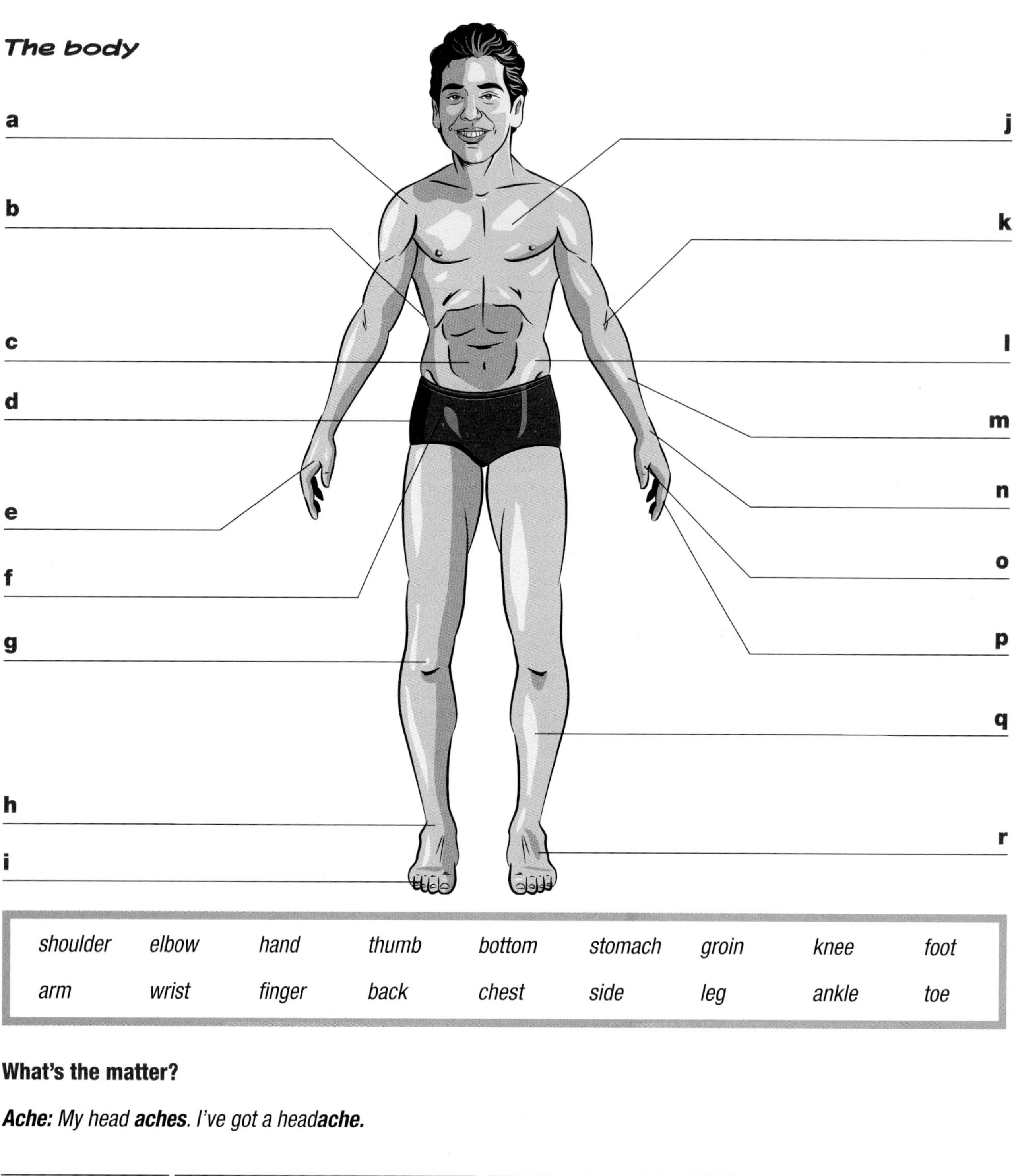

shoulder	elbow	hand	thumb	bottom	stomach	groin	knee	foot
arm	wrist	finger	back	chest	side	leg	ankle	toe

What's the matter?

Ache: *My head* ***aches****. I've got a head****ache.***

____________ ____________________ ____________________

My legs ***ache****. My knees* ***ache****. I* ***ache*** *all over.*

____________________ ____________________

Pain: *I've got a* ***pain*** *in my chest. I've got chest* ***pains****.*

____________ ____________________ ____________________

earache ____________________ *toothache* ____________________

neck ache ____________________ *shoulder ache* ____________________

backache ____________________ *stomachache* ____________________ *a pain in my stomach* ______________

a pain in my back ______________

a pain in my side ______________

a pain in my groin ______________

a pain in my leg ______________

Strain: *I've got* ***eyestrain*** *after driving all night.* ______ ______________

I've ***strained*** *my shoulder, my wrist, my knee, my ankle.*

____

14 Jobs

1 Do you know what these people do? Write the jobs in your own language.

accountant	______	*administrator*	______	*architect*	______
builder	______	*bus driver*	______	*businessman/woman*	______
carpenter	______	*civil engineer*	______	*cleaner*	______
designer	______	*electrician*	______	*IT specialist*	______
manager	______	*mechanic*	______	*plumber*	______
receptionist	______	*salesperson*	______	*shop assistant*	______
taxi driver	______	*teacher*	______	*technician*	______
travel agent	______	*web designer*	______		

2 Do you work full-time or part-time? Do you do shift work? Do you work unsocial hours?

____

____

____

15 Numbers

Cardinal numbers

1	one	2	two	3	three	4	four	5	five
6	six	7	seven	8	eight	9	nine	10	ten
11	eleven	12	twelve	13	thirteen	14	fourteen	15	fifteen
16	sixteen	17	seventeen	18	eighteen	19	nineteen	20	twenty
30	thirty	40	forty	50	fifty	60	sixty	70	seventy
80	eighty	90	ninety	100	a hundred	101	a hundred and one	22	twenty-two
33	thirty-three	44	forty-four	55	fifty-five	66	sixty-six	77	seventy-seven
88	eighty-eight	99	ninety-nine	1000	a thousand				

10,000 ten thousand

20,000 twenty thousand

33,000 thirty-three thousand

40,400 forty thousand, four hundred

500,000 five hundred thousand

1,000,000 a million

Ordinal numbers

1st first	11th eleventh	21st twenty-first
2nd second	12th twelfth	22nd twenty-second
3rd third	13th thirteenth	33rd thirty-third
4th fourth	14th fourteenth	44th forty-fourth
5th fifth	15th fifteenth	55th fifty-fifth
6th sixth	16th sixteenth	66th sixty-sixth
7th seventh	17th seventeenth	77th seventy-seventh
8th eighth	18th eighteenth	88th eighty-eighth
9th ninth	19th nineteenth	99th ninety-ninth
10th tenth	20th twentieth	100th one hundredth

Dates

02/02/08 = the second of February, two thousand and eight

14th July, 1966 – the fourteenth of July, nineteen sixty-six

How do we say these numbers and dates?

a *3* ________ **b** *14* ________

c *40* ________ **d** *22* ________

e *105* ________ **f** *97* ________

g *15,000* ________ **h** *432,000* ________

i *337* ________ **j** *3rd* ________

k *31st* ________ **l** *12th* ________

m *42nd* ________ **n** *101st* ________

o *03/03/2003* ________ **p** *14/07/1982* ________

16 Verbs

Regular verbs

/ɪd/		/d/		/t/	
present	**past**	**present**	**past**	**present**	**past**
carry	carried	arrive	arrived	cook	cooked
copy	copied	call	called	crash	crashed
decide	decided	clean	cleaned	finish	finished
hate	hated	close	closed	help	helped
need	needed	die	died	like	liked
start	started	enjoy	enjoyed	pick	picked
study	studied	live	lived	stop	stopped
visit	visited	love	loved	talk	talked
wait	waited	move	moved	walk	walked
		phone	phoned	wash	washed
		play	played	watch	watched
		reply	replied	work	worked
		stay	stayed		
		tried	tried		

Irregular verbs

infinitive	simple past	past participle	infinitive	simple past	past participle
be	was/were	been	light	lit	lit
become	became	become	lose	lost	lost
begin	began	begun	make	made	made
break	broke	broken	meet	met	met
bring	brought	brought	pay	paid	paid
build	built	built	put	put	put
buy	bought	bought	read	read	read
catch	caught	caught	ring	rang	rung
choose	chose	chosen	run	ran	run
come	came	come	say	said	said
cost	cost	cost	see	saw	seen
cut	cut	cut	sell	sold	sold
do	did	done	send	sent	sent
drink	drank	drunk	show	showed	shown
drive	drove	driven	shut	shut	shut
eat	ate	eaten	sing	sang	sung
fall	fell	fallen	sit	sat	sat
feel	felt	felt	sleep	slept	slept
find	found	found	speak	spoke	spoken
fly	flew	flown	spend	spent	spent
forget	forgot	forgotten	stand	stood	stood
freeze	froze	frozen	steal	stole	stolen
get	got	got	swim	swam	swum
give	gave	given	take	took	taken
go	went	gone/been	teach	taught	taught
grow	grew	grown	tell	told	told
have	had	had	think	thought	thought
hear	heard	heard	throw	threw	thrown
hit	hit	hit	understand	understood	understood
hold	held	held	wake	woke	woken
keep	kept	kept	wear	wore	worn
know	knew	known	win	won	won
leave	left	left	write	wrote	written
lend	lent	lent			
let	let	let			

17 Verbs + prepositions

to	belong to, listen to, speak to, talk to, write to
for	ask for (something), thank (someone) for (something), wait for
on	depend on, rely on
in	believe in

Phrasal verbs

up	*clean up* *get up* *hurry up* *look up* *pick up* *tidy up* *wash up*	make clean and tidy get out of bed be quick find information in a book or on the Internet, etc. collect someone from somewhere clean and make order in a place wash the dishes
on/off	*put on / take off* *turn on / off* *switch on / off*	dress and remove clothes put the power on or off put the power on or off
on	*come on* *go on*	be quick continue
for	*look for*	try to find someone or something that is missing
after	*look after*	take care of someone or something
at	*look at*	watch

18 The weather

Sun, wind, rain and cloud

The sun's shining. It's sunny. It's a sunny day. It's dry.

The wind's blowing. It's windy. It's a windy day.

It's raining. It's a rainy day. It's wet.

It's grey and cloudy. It's a cloudy day.

Temperature

Write the words in the correct places on the scale.

warm	*cold*	*hot*	*cool*	*freezing*	*boiling hot*	*mild*

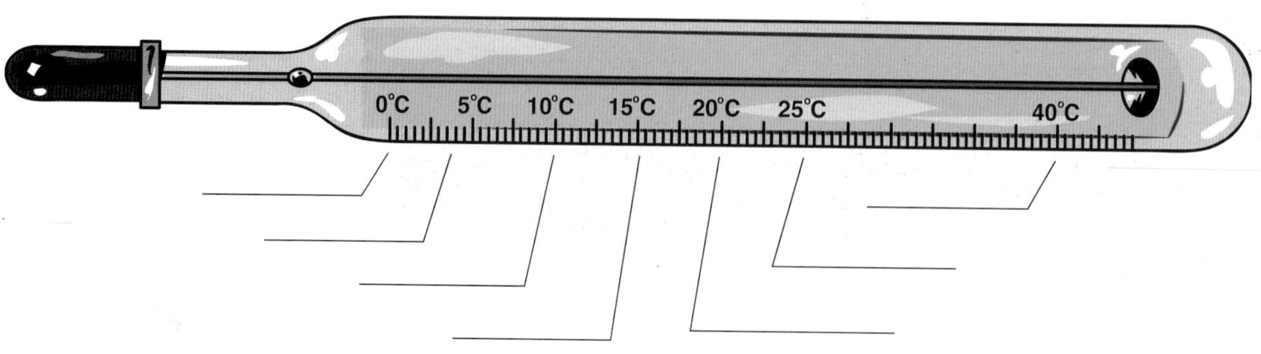

Unit 1

A

	Verb be long form	Verb be short form	Negative form
I	*I am*	*I'm*	*I'm not*
You	*You are*	*You're*	*You aren't / You're not*
He	*He is*	*He's*	*He isn't*
She	*She is*	*She's*	*She isn't*
It	*It is*	*It's*	*It isn't*
We	*We are*	*We're*	*We aren't / We're not*
They	*They are*	*They're*	*They aren't / They're not*

B

Question	Answers
Are you happy?	*Yes, I am.*
Are you single?	*No, I'm not.*
Are you single?	*Yes, I am.*
Are you English?	*No, I'm not.*
How old are you?	*I'm ______.*
Where are you from?	*I'm from ______.*
Is your friend English?	*Yes, she is.*
Is your friend single?	*No, she isn't.*
Is your car new?	*No, it isn't.*
Is your car very old?	*Yes, it is.*
Are your children very young?	*Yes, they are.*
Are your parents in England?	*No they aren't / they're not.*

1 **a** *I'm not* **b** *isn't* **c** *is* **d** *is*
e *isn't* **f** *aren't* **g** *I'm; I'm* **h** *is*
i *We're* **j** *Is* **k** *is*

2 **a** *8* **b** *9* **c** *6*
d *3* **e** *4* **f** *1*
g *2* **h** *7* **i** *5*

3 **a** *'m* **b** *isn't* **c** *is ('s)* **d** *'m*
e *'m* **f** *'m* **g** *'m* **h** *is ('s)*
i *is ('s)* **j** *is ('s)* **k** *are* **l** *are ('re)*
m *are ('re)* **n** *aren't ('re not)* **o** *are ('e).*

Unit 2

A **1** *There are* **2** *They are* **3** *There's* **4** *There's*
B *Yes, there are.*
No, there aren't.

1 **a** *is* **b** *There are* **c** *are some* **d** *isn't*
e *aren't any* **f** *There are some* **g** *Are; any*

2 **a** *There's a photo* **b** *There's a mobile phone*
c *There are some glasses* **d** *There are some keys*
e *There are some trainers* **f** *There's a book*
g *There are some DVDs*

3 **a** *6* **b** *5* **c** *7* **d** *8*
e *3* **f** *1* **g** *2* **h** *4*

Unit 3

A

I am (I'm)	*I'm not*	*learning English.*
You are (You're)	*You aren't*	*working.*
He is (He's)	*He isn't*	*looking for a job.*
She is (She's)	*She isn't*	*moving house.*
It is (It's)	*It isn't*	*raining.*
We are (We're)	*We aren't*	*shopping.*
They are (They're)	*They aren't*	*studying.*

B **1** *shopping* **2** *moving* **3** *studying*
C **1** *are; ing* **2** *Are; ing* **3** *Is; ing* **4** *Is; ing;* **5** *are; ing* **6** *are; ing*

1 **a** *talking* **b** *living* **c** *working* **d** *getting*
e *taking* **f** *walking* **g** *moving* **h** *driving*
i *coming* **j** *using* **k** *studying* **l** *shopping*
m *speaking* **n** *having* **o** *doing* **p** *phoning*
q *going* **r** *listening* **s** *eating* **t** *staying*

2 **a** *is ('s) watching* **b** *is ('s); going* **c** *am ('m) phoning* **d** *is ('s) starting*
e *isn't working* **f** *Are; using* **g** *are ('re) moving* **h** *are ('re) having*

3 **a** *Naomi's talking on the phone.* **b** *Jamie's reading a paper.*
c *Ali and Malik are laughing.* **d** *Dee's using a computer.*
e *Jan's eating a sandwich.* **f** *Beatriz is walking out / going out / leaving.*

4 **a** *Naomi isn't talking. She's drinking coffee.*
b *Jamie isn't reading. He's writing.*
c *Ali isn't laughing. He's eating a banana.*
d *Malik isn't talking to Ali. He's saying hello to Dee.*
e *Dee isn't using her computer. She's saying hello to Malik.*
f *Jan isn't eating a sandwich. He's reading a paper.*
g *Beatriz isn't walking out / going out / leaving. She's coming in with some shopping.*

Unit 4

A

I study	*I do not (don't) study*	*English.*
You work	*You <u>do</u> <u>not</u> (don't) work*	*part-time.*
We go	*We <u>do</u> <u>not</u> (<u>don't</u>) go*	*to the same college.*
They go	*They <u>do</u> <u>not</u> (<u>don't</u>) go*	*to work.*

B **a** *do* **b** *do* **c** *go* **d** *do* **e** *don't; work* **f** *they do*

1 **a** *Where* **b** *don't drive* **c** *Do you take*
d *live* **e** *do you speak* **f** *do they usually go*
g *don't* **h** *study; do* **i** *don't; drink*

2 **a** *don't* **b** *do; go* **c** *like; do*
d *drive* **e** *don't; They; look* **f** *Do; speak; No*

3 *Students' own answers.*

4 **a** *do you go* **b** *do you do* **c** *Do you do / play* **d** *do you live*
e *do you get up* **f** *Do you do* **g** *do you have*

Unit 5

A

He drives *He has*	*He does not (doesn't) drive* *He <u>does</u> <u>not</u> (doesn't) <u>have</u>*	*a taxi.* *a job.*
She <u>teaches</u>	*She <u>does</u> <u>not</u> (doesn't) teach*	*at university.*
It <u>rains</u>	*It <u>does</u> <u>not</u> (<u>doesn't</u>) rain*	*a lot in England.*

B **1** *Does; does* **2** *have* **3** *does; teaches* **4** *Does; does*

1
a *likes* **b** *teaches* **c** *studies* **d** *rains*
e *drives* **f** *goes* **g** *flies* **h** *learns*
i *moves* **j** *does* **k** *carries* **l** *reads*
m *lives* **n** *finishes* **o** *cries* **p** *listens*
q *comes* **r** *washes* **s** *buys* **t** *takes*

2 ***one sound:*** *drives, goes, flies, lives, moves, does, reads, learns, cries, comes, buys, takes*
two sounds: *studies, carries, listens, washes*
three sounds: *finishes*

3
a *comes* **b** *Does* **c** *doesn't* **d** *have*
e *get* **f** *play* **g** *does; start* **h** *Does he take*
i *doesn't listen*

4
a *he gets up* **b** *he usually gets up* **c** *He usually works* **d** *He has*
e *drives* **f** *starts* **g** *He usually has* **h** *he goes*
i *He takes* **j** *He finishes* **k** *he works* **l** *he gets up*
m *he doesn't get* **n** *he doesn't have* **o** *He likes*

Unit 6

B **1** *Turn* **2** *walk* **3** *Cross* **4** *take* **5** *Don't take*

1
a *Turn* **b** *Don't call* **c** *answer* **d** *Don't take*
e *Finish* **f** *Phone* **g** *fill*

2
a *2* **b** *7* **c** *9* **d** *1*
e *4* **f** *3* **g** *6* **h** *5*
i *8*

3
a *go* **b** *Stay* **c** *Don't get up* **d** *Take*
e *Drink* **f** *don't eat* **g** *Don't go* **h** *Call*

Unit 7

A **1** *Where* **2** *How* **3** *Which* **4** *When* **5** *Who* **6** *Whose* **7** *Why*

1
a *are* **b** *What* **c** *How* **d** *Why*
e *When* **f** *Whose* **g** *How often*

2 **a** *9* **b** *4* **c** *5* **d** *6*
e *7* **f** *2* **g** *3* **h** *1*
i *8*

3 **a** *What* **b** *How* **c** *Whose* **d** *Why*
e *When/What time* **f** *Which* **g** *Where* **h** *How*
i *Who*

4 **a** *How old are you?*
b *What do you do? / What's your job?*
c *When / What time do you get up?*
d *What do you have for breakfast?*
e *Who do you live with?*
f *Why do you want to learn English?*
g *Which colour do you prefer?*
h *How do you spell your name?*
i *How often do you work?*
j *Whose car is that?*

5 **a** ✓
b *Whose car*
c *When does*
d ✓
e *Where is*

Unit 8

A **1** *I can't; Can you* **2** *can; Can I; I can't make; I could come*

1 **a** *understand* **b** *I can* **c** *Can you* **d** *see*
e *can't* **f** *Could I* **g** *couldn't* **h** *I can*
i *ask*

2 **a** *Can* **b** *can* **c** *can't* **d** *can*
e *can't* **f** *Can; can't* **g** *can; can't (can't; can)*

3 **a** *couldn't* **b** *could* **c** *couldn't*
d *could; couldn't* **e** *could* **f** *could*

4 **a** *Could you post this letter, please?*
b *Could I use your phone, please?*
c *Could you repeat your address, please?*
d *Could you turn down the television, please?*
e *Could I borrow your dictionary, please?*

5 *Can you speak a third language?*
Can you ride a camel?
Can you cook?
Can you draw?
Can you play the guitar?
Can you ride a bike?
Can you make a cake?

Unit 9

A *We've / They've / I've got; Have we got; I've / We've got; It's got*
B **1** *Have; got; have* **2** *Has; got; hasn't*

1 **a** *haven't got* **b** *has got* **c** *Have you got* **d** *have*
e *hasn't got* **f** *hasn't* **g** *they've got* **h** *Has he got*
i *has*

2 **a** *She's got toothache.* **b** *He's got neck ache.*
c *She's got a headache.* **d** *She's got an earache.*
e *He's got a stomachache.* **f** *They've got colds.*

3 **a** *Have you got; have; I've got* **b** *Have we got; have;*
c *Has she got; has; She's got* **d** *Has it got; hasn't got*
e *Have you got; haven't* **f** *Has he got; hasn't*
g *Have they got; haven't*

4 **a** *have ('ve) got* **b** *haven't got*
c *hasn't got* **d** *has ('s) got; has ('s) got*
e *have ('ve) got; haven't got* **f** *have ('ve) got; haven't got*
g *have ('ve) got; hasn't got*

Unit 10

A **1** *some; some; some* **2** *any; any* **3** *any* **4** *some; some; Yes*

1 **a** *some* **b** *any* **c** *any* **d** *any*
e *some* **f** *some* **g** *any; any* **h** *anything*
i *any; any*

2 **a** *some* **b** *any* **c** *any* **d** *some*
e *any* **f** *any* **g** *some* **h** *some*
i *any*

3 *(a–c, in any order) some houses, cats, people talking.*
(d–g, in any order) any gardens, trees, shops, children playing.

4 **a** *some* **b** *any* **c** *any* **d** *some*
e *any* **f** *any; any* **g** *some* **h** *any*
i *any; any*

Unit 11

A 1 ***With nouns we can count, we use*** how many? How many *eggs shall we get?* ***We use*** a lot ***for a large quantity****. I want to make* a lot *of cakes.* ***We use*** a few ***or not*** many ***for a small quantity.*** *Only* a few. *We don't need* many.

2 ***With nouns we can't count, we use how*** much? How much *milk shall we get?* ***We use*** a lot ***for a large quantity.*** *We need* a lot, *so get a couple of big bottles.* ***We use*** a little ***or not*** much ***for a small quantity.*** *Just* a little. *We don't use* much.

1 ***How much? / a little****: money; time; coffee; petrol; orange juice; cash; sugar; information; English; sport; cola; meat; exercise; salad*
How many? / a few*: lessons; times; students; children; tables; oranges; pounds; sports; onions; flowers*

2 **a** *students / children* **b** *money / cash*
c *students / children / tables / flowers* **d** *English / information*
e *meat / salad* **f** *oranges / onions*
g *sport / exercise / English* **h** *times*
i *time*

3 **a** *eggs / apples / sandwiches* **b** *orange juice / lettuce*
c *orange juice / lettuce / cheese* **d** *eggs / apples / sandwiches*
e *cola* **f** *cheese / orange juice*
g *eggs / apples / sandwiches*

4 **1** *little* **2** *many; lot* **3** *much; lot* **4** *many; few; many*
5 *much; little; much* **6** *many; many*

5 **a** *a little* **b** *How much* **c** *a lot*
d *a few* **e** *How many*

Unit 12

A **1** *cars; streets* **2** *buses* **3** *babies; boys* **4** *wives*
5 *men; people; children* **6** *sunglasses* **7** *traffic*

1 **a** *watches* **b** *ladies* **c** *days* **d** *knives*
e *teeth* **f** *trousers* **g** – **h** *bags*
i *banks* **j** *boxes* **k** *cities* **l** *mice*
m *sandwiches* **n** *eggs* **o** *churches* **p** *weeks*
q – **r** *shorts* **s** *cameras* **t** *families*
u *gentlemen*

2 **a** *woman* **b** *house* **c** *dish* **d** *fish*
e *class* **f** *person* **g** *loaf* **h** *party*
i *foot* **j** *sheep* **k** *child*

3 **a** ✓ **b** *keys* **c** *food* **d** ✓ **e** *information*
f *some new pyjamas* **g** ✓ **h** *There are* **i** *people*

4 **a** *milk; bottles, milk* **b** *eggs; A dozen eggs*
c *Some pyjamas; A pair of pyjamas* **d** *sugar; spoonfuls; sugar*
e *feet; Two pairs of feet* **f** *people; A group of people*

Unit 13

A **1** *a* **2** *an; an* **3** *an hour* **4** *university*
5 *The; the; The university; the countryside; The office; the city*

1 **a** *a* **b** *an* **c** *a* **d** *a* **e** *an*
f *a* **g** *an* **h** *a* **i** *an* **j** *a*
k *an* **l** *a* **m** *a* **n** *an* **o** *an*
p *a* **q** *a* **r** *a* **s** *an*

2 **a** *an electrician* **b** *The food*
c *an hour* **d** *the time*
e *the University Hospital; a nurse* **f** *a nice house; The house; a garden*
g *the new film; the cinema*

3 **a** *6 An actor works in a (the) theatre.* **b** *4 A waiter works in a restaurant.*
c *1 A lion is an animal.* **d** *7 A chicken is a bird.*
e *8 An artist works in a studio.* **f** *2 A dolphin lives in the sea.*
g *5 A plane lands at an airport.* **h** *3 A doctor works in a hospital.*

4 *a; an; a; an; a / the; a; a; an; the; the; the; the*

Unit 14

A *towns and cities; countries; stations and airports; schools and colleges; college subjects*
B **1** *fruit; vegetables; salt; fat; sugar* **2** *The children*

1 **a** – **b** – **c** – **d** *The* **e** –
f *The* **g** *The* **h** – **i** – **j** –
k *The* **l** – **m** *The* **n** –

2 **a** *The talk was interesting.* **b** *The car drove up the road.* **c** *The flowers were beautiful.* **d** *I sat by the window.* **e** *She ate the cake.*

3 **a** – **b** *the* **c** – **d** – **e** *The* **f** – **g** *The* **h** – **i** – **j** *The* **k** – **l** *the*

4 *Students' own answers.*

Unit 15

A **1** *this; these* **2** *that; those*

1 **a** *this* **b** *those* **c** *these* **d** *this* **e** *This* **f** *that; This* **g** *those* **h** *This* **i** *that*

2 **a** *these* **b** *that* **c** *this* **d** *those* **e** *this* **f** *these* **g** *that*

3 **a** *This* **b** *this; that* **c** *that* **d** *those* **e** *That* **f** *those* **g** *this* **h** *This* **i** *these*

Unit 16

A

Subject	Object	Possessive	
I've got a flat.	*It belongs to <u>me</u>.*	*It's <u>my</u> flat.*	*It's <u>mine</u>.*
<u>You</u>'ve got a flat.	*It belongs to you.*	*It's <u>your</u> flat.*	*It's yours.*
He's got a flat.	*It belongs to him.*	*It's <u>his</u> flat.*	*It's his.*
She's got a garden.	*It belongs to her.*	*It's <u>her</u> garden.*	*It's hers.*
<u>We</u>'ve got a house.	*It belongs to <u>us</u>.*	*It's our house.*	*It's ours.*
They've got a house.	*It belongs to them.*	*It's their house.*	*It's <u>theirs</u>.*

1 **a** *He* **b** *She* **c** *I* **d** *We* **e** *They*

2 **a** *them* **b** *him* **c** *us* **d** *her*

3 **a** *your* **b** *her* **c** *his* **d** *their*

4 **a** *hers* **b** *yours; mine* **c** *ours* **d** *theirs*

5 **a** *me; your* **b** *His; my* **c** *her; mine* **d** *us; our* **e** *Our; their*

Unit 17

A **1** *blue; old; new*
2 *tall; good-looking; happy; good*

1 **a** *I've got some new shoes.* **b** *These eggs are fresh.* **c** *She is wearing blue jeans.* **d** *This is my youngest daughter.* **e** *There are black clouds in the sky.*

2 **a** *The weather is fine.* **b** *This room feels cold.* **c** *I am not happy.* **d** *She doesn't feel hungry.* **e** *The job sounds interesting.*

3 **a** *poor people* **b** *beautiful flowers* **c** *looks very young* **d** *I am very hungry.* **e** *feeling happy*

4 **a** *She is hungry.* **b** *It tastes terrible.* **c** *He feels sad.* **d** *They smell lovely.* **e** *Your news sounds exciting.* **f** *She looks beautiful.*

Unit 18

A **1** *slowly; badly; easily* **2** *well; fast; hard*

1 **a** *slowly* **b** *quickly* **c** *happily* **d** *carefully* **e** *quietly* **f** *angrily* **g** *fast* **h** *badly* **i** *well* **j** *hard* **k** *heavily* **l** *dangerously* **m** *seriously* **n** *safely* **o** *strongly*

2 **a** ✓ **b** *Please speak slowly.* **c** ✓ **d** ✓ **e** *Cheng works hard at his English.* **f** *Petra laughs happily.* **g** ✓ **h** *Hamid plays tennis very well.* **i** ✓

3 *Students' own answers.*

5 **a** *5* **b** *4* **c** *1* **d** *6* **e** *2* **f** *3*

Unit 19

1 **a** *on* **b** *in* **c** *on* **d** *in* **e** *at* **f** *in* **g** *at* **h** *in* **i** *in* **j** *on* **k** *at* **l** *at* **m** *on* **n** *on*

2 **a** *at; at* **b** *at; on* **c** *in* **d** *at* **e** *on*

3 **a** *at; in* **b** *at; in; on* **c** *On; at; in* **d** *on; at; in* **e** *On; at; in; on* **f** *On; at; in*

Unit 20

1 **a** *3* **b** *7* **c** *6* **d** *8* **e** *4* **f** *1* **g** *2* **h** *5*

2 **a** *in* **b** *in* **c** *in* **d** *on* **e** *at* **f** *in* **g** *on* **h** *at* **i** *at*

3 **a** *on* **b** *in* **c** *in; in* **d** *at* **e** *on* **f** *at (in)*

Unit 21

1
a *Yes, it is.*
b *Yes, it is.*
c *No, it doesn't. It goes under the bridge.*
d *No, there isn't. It's in front of the bank.*
e *No, it isn't. It's next to the chemist's.*
f *Yes, it is.*
g *No, it isn't. It's on the right.*
h *Yes, it is.*
i *No, it isn't. It's behind the supermarket.*
j *No, it isn't. It's behind the bank.*

2
a *It's next to the supermarket, behind the bank.*
b *The doctor's surgery is behind the supermarket.*
c *The chemist's is between the post office and the café.*
d *Yes, it's in front of the bank.*
e *The bank is next to the supermarket.*
f *Yes, it's next to the chemist's.*
g *The post office is on the right of the chemist's, opposite the bank.*
h *Yes, the park is behind the supermarket.*

3 **a** *in front of* **b** *behind* **c** *under*
d *by (near); on the* **e** *behind; on the right* **f** *in the middle, between*
g *facing (opposite)*

Unit 22

1 **a** *3* **b** *7* **c** *8* **d** *6* **e** *1* **f** *5* **g** *4* **h** *2*

2 **a** *gets home* **b** *go to work* **c** *get to work* **d** *works at home*
e *go to bed* **f** *get on the train* **g** *by bus*

3 **a** *by* **b** *at* **c** *–* **d** *on*
e *in* **f** *on*

Unit 23

1 **a** *to* **b** *for* **c** *to* **d** *up*
e *on* **f** *off* **g** *up* **h** *after*

2 **a** *washes* **b** *turns* **c** *writes* **d** *depends*
e *tidies* **f** *belongs* **g** *takes*

3 **a** *on* **b** *for* **c** *on* **d** *to*
e *on* **f** *for* **g** *up*

Unit 24

A **1** *do* **2** *Would you like* **3** *What is it like*

1
1 *d, f, h*
2 *b, c, i, j*
3 *a, e, g, k*

2 **a** *3* **b** *5* **c** *8* **d** *6* **e** *1*
f *4* **g** *2* **h** *7*

3 **a** *Do* **b** *Do* **c** *Would* **d** *Do* **e** *would*

4 **a** *is ('s); like; It is (It's)* **b** *What are; like; They are / They're* **c** *What was; like; It, was* **d** *What was; like; It was* **e** *(What's) What is; like; He is (He's)*

Unit 25

A **1** *weren't; was; were; weren't* **2** *Were; Was; Were; Were*

1 **a** *were* **b** *wasn't* **c** *Were* **d** *was* **e** *were* **f** *wasn't* **g** *was*

2 **a** *My mother was pleased to see me.* **b** *The weather wasn't sunny on holiday.* **c** *The shopping bill wasn't correct.* **d** *Were you tired after your journey?* **e** *Was she happy in her country?* **f** *Were they busy yesterday?* **g** *Was Jan in class on Wednesday?*

3 **a** *was; was* **b** *Was; wasn't; was* **c** *Were; weren't; were* **d** *Was; was; was* **e** *Was; wasn't; was* **f** *Were; weren't; were* **g** *Was; was; was* **h** *Was; wasn't; was*

Unit 26

A **1** *started* **2** *didn't come* **3** *Did; study* **4** *did*

1 /ɪd/: *visited; started; needed; hated; decided; copied*
/d/: *lived; phoned; arrived; died; moved; closed; called; cleaned; replied; stayed*
/t/: *watched; washed; crashed; finished; walked; talked; worked; picked; cooked; helped; liked; dropped*

2 **a** ✓ **b** ✓ **c** *enjoy* **d** ✓ **e** *He didn't live* **f** *did you finish* **g** ✓

3 **a** *did; studied* **b** *did; arrived* **c** *didn't; rained* **d** *did; helped* **e** *did, talked*

4 **a** *Did; phone* **b** *did; stay* **c** *did; cook* **d** *did; decide* **e** *Did; walk*

Unit 27

A **1** *went; saw; met; flew* **2** *didn't get* **3** *Did; have* **4** *did*

1 **a** *did* **b** *came* **c** *got* **d** *gave* **e** *took*
f *left* **g** *sold* **h** *drove* **i** *understood* **j** *made*
k *ate* **l** *slept* **m** *put* **n** *thought* **o** *read*
p *told* **q** *spoke* **r** *bought* **s** *sat*

2 **a** *spoke* **b** *know*
c *did; got* **d** *did; do*
e *Did; didn't understand* **f** *Did; did; didn't drive; went*

3 **a** *had; did; go; went; did; do; saw; made; went; swam*
b *did; do; didn't do; went; saw; Did; go; slept; got; had; did; went*

Unit 28

A **1** *'ll; go; won't; 'll see* **2** *'re going to have; 'm going to stay*
3 *are; doing; 'm meeting; are; coming; 'm taking*

1 **a** *4* **b** *6* **c** *1* **d** *5* **e** *3*
f *2* **g** *7*

2 **a** *'s going to* **b** *'re going to* **c** *'s going to* **d** *'s going to* **e** *'re going to*

3 *'m going; 's taking; 'm staying; 's picking; 's looking; are; coming; are; going*

Unit 29

A **1** *must / have to; must / have to* **2** *don't have to* **3** *mustn't* **4** *didn't have to; had to*

1 **a** *I must check my e-mails.*
b *You mustn't phone the office before 9 a.m.*
c *I have to wear special clothes in my job.*
d *When I was at school, I had to wear a uniform.*
e *He doesn't have to travel in his job.*
f *You mustn't smoke in restaurants in England.*
g *I didn't have to pay for the coffee because my friend paid for me.*

2 **a** *3* **b** *7* **c** *1* **d** *8*
e *6* **f** *2* **g** *5* **h** *4*

3 **a** *mustn't* **b** *don't have to* **c** *don't have to* **d** *mustn't*
e *mustn't* **f** *don't have to*

4 **a** *mustn't* **b** *do; have; have* **c** *have to; must* **d** *Do; have to; must*
e *have to; didn't have* **f** *Did; have to; had to*

Unit 30

A **1** *warmer; bigger* **2** *busier* **3** *more comfortable; more expensive; more beautiful* **4** *better; worse*
5 *than; than*

1 *Short adjectives + ~er: darker; older; nearer; younger; shorter*
Short adjectives, double consonant: hotter; fatter; sadder; slimmer; fitter
Adjectives ending with ~y: angrier; heavier; friendlier; easier
Long adjectives: more comfortable; more important; more serious; more dangerous; more careful; more interesting

2 **a** *faster* **b** *more careful* **c** *than mine* **d** *better*
e *is nicer* **f** *worse* **g** *than my old one*

3 **a** *taller than* **b** *more serious than* **c** *better; than* **d** *works harder than*
e *is more careful than* **f** *is happier than*

Database

1.1 ***Do:*** *the cooking, the housework, homework, the cleaning, exercise, the washing*
Go: *swimming, jogging, fishing, travelling*

4

a *a cheese roll*	**b** *an orange juice*	**c** *a muffin*
d *a piece of cake*	**e** *a mug of tea*	**f** *a toasted sandwich*
g *a chicken salad sandwich*	**h** *a cappuccino*	**i** *a jacket potato*
j *a milkshake*	**k** *a baguette with egg mayo*	**l** *a black coffee*

5 **a** *T-shirt, jeans, belt, socks, trainers* **b** *blouse, sweater, skirt, tights, slippers*
c *shirt, tie, jacket, trousers, shoes*

8.1

a *7*	**b** *5*	**c** *10*	**d** *2*	**e** *12*
f *1*	**g** *11*	**h** *6*	**i** *3*	**j** *8*
k *9*	**l** *4*			

8.3

a *Egypt*	**b** *India*	**c** *Pakistan*	**d** *Sudan*	**e** *Somalia*
f *Brazil*	**g** *Taiwan*	**h** *Russia*	**i** *Morocco*	**j** *Thailand*
k *The Philippines*	**l** *Saudi Arabia*	**m** *Iraq*	**n** *Japan*	**o** *America*
p *Colombia*	**q** *Argentina*	**r** *Indonesia*		

9.1 *Wednesday 3; Saturday 6; Monday 1; Friday 5; Sunday 7; Tuesday 2; Thursday 4*

9.2 *September 9; January 1; December 12; March 3; July 7; February 2; October 10; August 8; April 4; June 6; November 11; May 5*

11.1 ***Meat:***

a *chicken*	**b** *lamb*	**c** *turkey*	**d** *pork, ham, bacon*
e *veal*	**f** *beef*		

Fruit:

a *banana*	**b** *lemon*	**c** *blackberry*	**d** *strawberry*
e *peach*	**f** *cherry*	**g** *fig*	**h** *apple*
i *grapes*	**j** *dates*	**k** *apricot*	**l** *pear*
m *orange*	**n** *pineapple*	**o** *melon*	**p** *raspberry*

Vegetables:

a *broccoli*	**b** *onion*	**c** *cauliflower*	**d** *lettuce*
e *cabbage*	**f** *potato*	**g** *peas*	**h** *tomato*
i *avocado*	**j** *beans*	**k** *leek*	**l** *cucumber*

12.1

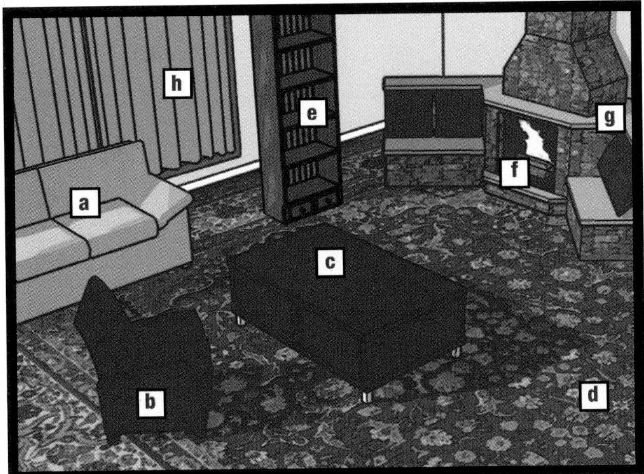

12.2

13 The face

a *head* **b** *hair* **c** *eye* **d** *nose*
e *teeth* **f** *lips* **g** *eyebrow* **h** *ear*
i *cheek* **j** *chin* **k** *neck* **l** *throat*

The body

a *shoulder* **b** *back* **c** *stomach* **d** *bottom* **e** *hand* **f** *groin* **g** *knee*
h *ankle* **i** *toe* **j** *chest* **k** *elbow* **l** *side* **m** *arm* **n** *wrist*
o *thumb* **p** *finger* **q** *leg* **r** *foot*

15 **a** *three* **b** *fourteen* **c** *forty* **d** *twenty-two* **e** *a hundred and five* **f** *ninety-seven*
g *fifteen thousand* **h** *four hundred and thirty-two thousand* **i** *three hundred and thirty-seven*
j *third* **k** *thirty-first* **l** *twelfth* **m** *forty-second* **n** *a hundred and first*
o *the third of March two thousand and three* **p** *the fourteenth of July nineteen eighty-two*

18 *freezing, cold, cool, mild, warm, hot, boiling hot*

Key to pronunciation

Short vowels

ɪ	***i**s*
e	*g**e**t*
æ	*c**a**t*
ʌ	*s**u**n*
ɒ	*h**o**t*
ʊ	*f**oo**t, p**u**t*
ə	***a**pply*

Long vowels

ɑː	***ar**m, c**al**m*
iː	*w**e**, s**ee***
uː	*wh**o**, y**ou***
ɔː	*f**our**, s**aw***
ɜː	*b**ir**d, l**ear**n, w**or**d*

Diphthongs

eɪ	*d**ay**, th**ey***
aɪ	*f**i**ve, wh**y***
ɔɪ	*b**oy**, p**oi**nt*
əʊ	*h**o**me, n**o***
aʊ	*h**ou**se, n**ow***
ɪə	***ear**, h**ere***
eə	*h**air**, wh**ere***
ʊə	*p**oor**, t**our***
aɪə	*f**ire***
aʊə	*fl**ower***

Consonants

b	***b**ed*
d	***d**o*
f	***f**un*
g	***g**o*
h	***h**ouse*
k	***c**at*
l	***l**ook*
m	***m**an*
n	***n**o*
p	***p**ound*
r	***r**un*
s	***s**it*
t	***t**alk*
v	***v**an*
w	***w**ill*
z	***z**ebra*
tʃ	***ch**ip*
dʒ	***j**am*
x	*lo**ch***
ŋ	*ri**ng***
θ	***th**ink*
ð	***th**is*
ʃ	***sh**e*
ʒ	*deci**s**ion*
j	***y**es*